DECENTRALIZATION
& ITS DISCONTENTS

The **Institute of Southeast Asian Studies (ISEAS)** was established as an autonomous organization in 1968. It is a regional centre dedicated to the study of socio-political, security and economic trends and developments in Southeast Asia and its wider geostrategic and economic environment. The Institute's research programmes are the Regional Economic Studies (RES, including ASEAN and APEC), Regional Strategic and Political Studies (RSPS), and Regional Social and Cultural Studies (RSCS).

ISEAS Publishing, an established academic press, has issued more than 2,000 books and journals. It is the largest scholarly publisher of research about Southeast Asia from within the region. ISEAS Publishing works with many other academic and trade publishers and distributors to disseminate important research and analyses from and about Southeast Asia to the rest of the world.

ISEAS MONOGRAPH SERIES

DECENTRALIZATION & ITS DISCONTENTS

AN ESSAY ON CLASS, POLITICAL AGENCY AND NATIONAL PERSPECTIVE IN INDONESIAN POLITICS

MAX LANE

ISEAS

INSTITUTE OF SOUTHEAST ASIAN STUDIES
Singapore

First published in Singapore in 2014 by
ISEAS Publishing
Institute of Southeast Asian Studies
30 Heng Mui Keng Terrace
Pasir Panjang
Singapore 119614

E-mail: publish@iseas.edu.sg
Website: <http://bookshop.iseas.edu.sg>

ISEAS Library Cataloguing-in-Publication Data

Lane, Max, 1951–
   Decentralization and its discontents : an essay on class, political agency and national perspective in Indonesian politics.
   1. Decentralization in government—Indonesia.
   2. Indonesia—Economic policy—20th century.
   3. Capitalists and financiers—Indonesia.
   4. Indonesia—Politics and government—1998–
   I. Title.
   II. Title: Essay on class, political agency and national perspective in Indonesian politics.
JS7193 A2L26   2014

ISBN 978-981-4519-73-1 (hard cover)
ISBN 978-981-4519-74-8 (e-book, PDF)

Cover photo: Indonesian workers demonstrating on 3 September 2012.
Source: Reproduced with kind permission of Sherr Rinn.

Typeset by Superskill Graphics Pte Ltd
Printed in Singapore by Mainland Press Pte Ltd

Contents

Editorial Note

The ISEAS Monograph Series disseminates profound analyses by major scholars on key issues relating to Southeast Asia. Subjects studied in this series stem from research facilitated by the Institute of Southeast Asian Studies, Singapore.

The Institute's Manuscript Review Committee is in charge of the series, although the responsibility for facts presented and views expressed rests exclusively with the individual author or authors. No part of this publication may be reproduced in any form without permission from the Institute.

*****

Preface

This extended essay was written in late 2013 and early 2014, before the April 2014 election campaigns. One of the first lines written was: "There is a certain Jokowimania afoot". The March announcement by Megawati Sukarnoputri that the Indonesian Democratic Party of Struggle (PDI-P) would nominate Joko Widodo as its presidential candidate has accentuated this. Media coverage — including the social media — has narrowed down the formal political struggle for governmental power as one between Widodo, the *kabupaten* (district) capitalist, and Prabowo Subianto, representing the billionaire Djojohadikusumo family. At a certain level, it is a fight between *kabupaten* capitalism and crony capitalism, although there is no doubt much more behind this.

The emergence of a *kabupaten* capitalist as a presidential candidate, without doubt, has been possible as a direct result of the last ten years of decentralization, especially providing guaranteed funds over which local government can exercise some autonomy, giving local mayors and *bupati* greater room to nuance and market the implementation of policies as their own (when in fact such policies originated with international financial institutions working through the national government). The institution of direct elections for mayors and *bupati* has accentuated this trend. In decentralized Indonesia, Widodo has gone from head of the local businessmen's association, to mayor of a medium-sized town in Java, to governor of the province of Jakarta, and now, to being a presidential candidate of the Republic of Indonesia. He has done this through the PDI-P in a period when the PDI-P no longer has an obvious presence of big capitalists and former cronies in its ranks. The PDI-P is more perceived as being associated with other "rising stars" in regional politics, such as the mayor of Surabaya, "Ibu Risma" (Tri Rismaharini) and the governor of Central Java, Ganjar Pranowo.

Writing this preface before the 9 April 2014 elections, it is tempting to predict results. While it is likely that Widodo's candidacy will increase the vote for the PDI-P, at least a little, it remains the case that it is unlikely that there will be any one party or serious coalition of parties, which will be able to claim that it represents a majority of the population. The highest polling result for the PDI-P as of 2 April is 33 per cent. PDI-P is more often scoring around 25 per cent. All of the other parties score under 20 per cent, most under 10 per cent. Golkar and Gerindra score between 10–15 per cent in most polls. The percentage refusing to vote will still be high for the parliamentary elections — although it may drop substantially in July for the presidential elections.

The inability of parties to claim to represent a significant section of the public stems not only from their low percentage support. It also stems from an absence of political campaigning for or against anything. The election campaign, especially the national messaging through the media, has been empty of content. Widodo's main claim is that he is "electable"; there has not been, so far, any interrogation of his record or his policies, or the policies of his party. Prabowo's situation is slightly different. Prabowo struggles to claim electability with all of the polls against him, so his emphasis has been on his claims to being a "strong leader", in the style of a military campaigner, giving rise to increased criticims of militarism from some quarters.

This essay points to the end of (direct) crony capitalism at the national level and the shift in the possibility of political initiative to the *kabupaten* capitalists, and the initiatives can be different or even contradictory among local capitalists. It raises questions as to whether a new national socio-political agency for progressive change might emerge via the *kabupaten* capitalists and through the PDI-P . The essay speculates in the negative. The emptiness of the election campaign to date — and the emptiness of all the pre-announcement manoeuvres of 2013 — would seem to confirm this negative conclusion. The essay points to the labour movement as having greater potential, although that arena is also full of complications.

Max Lane
4 April 2014, Jakarta

About the Author

Max Lane is the author of *Unfinished Nation: Indonesia Before and After Suharto* (2008) and *Catastrophe in Indonesia* (2010). Both books have been translated into Indonesian. He is also translator of five novels and one non-fiction work by Pramoedya Ananta Toer, including the *Buru Tetralogy*, starting with *This Earth of Mankind*. He also translated the plays and poems of W.S. Rendra, including *The Struggle of the Naga Tribe*, to be republished in 2015.

Lane has also written hundreds of articles on Indonesia, the Philippines, Timor Leste and Australia for magazines and newspapers, mainly in Indonesia and Australia. He maintains a blog — maxlaneonline.com. He has worked in the Australian Department of Foreign Affairs, the Australian Parliament, *Green Left Weekly* newspaper, and as national coordinator for Action in Solidarity with Indonesia and East Timor.

He has been lecturing at Victoria University, Melbourne, for the last five years. He also lectures regularly at Gadjah Mada University and the State University of Yogyakarta. He has guest-lectured in universities in the United States, the Netherlands and the Philippines, among others. He is currently a Visiting Fellow with the Institute of Southeast Asian Studies, Singapore.

Introduction

Approaches to Understanding Indonesian Politics and Decentralization

It is very possible that the next president of Indonesia will be a former mayor from a modest size Central Javanese city: Joko Widodo, the mayor of Solo from 2005 to 2012. He was elected to the position of Governor of Jakarta in 2012, with 38 per cent of the vote in the first round and 56 per cent of the vote in the second round. His opponent, Fauzi Bowo, was supported by President Yudhoyono and the coalition of ruling parties. Whether Widodo is indeed nominated by the party he joined in 2004, namely the PDI-P (Partai Demokrasi Indonesia – Perjuangan, or Indonesian Democratic Party of Struggle), and then wins or some other scenario evolves, his stakes in the race are high. In September 2013, at a national working conference of the PDI-P, chaired by party head Megawati Sukarnoputri, Widodo emerged as its "star", with wide media discussion of his presidential prospects.

There is a kind of Jokowimania afoot.

How is it that a local furniture factory owner and local mayor, with no prior political record and no known views on most national issues, can rocket into this position? Has *"desentralisasi"* created a launching pad for a local politician to launch into national politics? This essay will argue that the rise of Jokowi and *desentralisasi* are connected, but *not as cause and effect*. It will argue that *both* are the results (effects) of other major changes, based in the political economy (the economic-based structure of political power). The essay will identify two major processes of change at work here.[1]

The first of these processes has longer term origins: namely, the quantitative growth of the Indonesian economy as a non-industrializing capitalist economy under authoritarian rule, resulting in a domestic capitalist class comprising a small number of politically protected big crony capitalists and *a huge number of small, local capitalists*. The inability to industrialize, due to the lack of any sizeable capital in the hands of either the state or private business at the time of independence in 1945 has, in turn, limited the post-independence capital accumulation, including since 1965. Neither the state nor Indonesian domestic capitalists have been able to develop late twentieth century scale industry anywhere near sufficient to begin to raise Indonesia's average labour productivity or general prosperity. This has had major ramifications for class structure. It has prevented the growth of a capitalist class which owns and runs investments that have a truly national scale, building a national industrial base and national market. There are such capitalists, but very few. Rather, Indonesia's capitalist class is overwhelmingly comprised of local (district and provincial level) small capitalists. It has a domestic, but hardly a national, capitalist class. I will discuss this further later in the essay.

The second process is constituted by the forced resignation of President Suharto, the end of authoritarian rule and its ability to protect the extraordinary privileges of the big crony businessmen. This development was primarily the result of rising public discontent manifested in escalating mass mobilizations.[2] As I will discuss later, the end of crony capitalism also saw a brief interregnum of technocratic rule under President Habibie from

May 1998 until November 1999. This role of the technocratic elements within the government and elite was strengthened by a synergy with international financial institution "donor" technocracies who saw decentralization as an element in their package of "transparency" and "good governance", as the post-Washington Consensus mechanism to ameliorate excesses of neo-liberal economic policy.

This essay is an initial exploration of a different argument: that decentralization is a result (effect) of these two processes intersecting with each other since 1998. One of several factors that will be explored in this essay will be the proposition that it is also the working through of this intersection that has facilitated the emergence of a figure such as Joko Widodo. While arguing for a particular explanation of the decentralization phenomenon, it does not aim to provide a final, documented picture of the phenomenon and all its aspects. Rather, the aim of the essay is to open a new discussion, with a new approach on this and other associated questions.

Understanding the nature of the phenomenon is necessary if there is also to be a realistic assessment of prospects and the conditions necessary for achieving the optimal benefits from the devolution of power to social progress and economic development, assuming that decentralization can actually be encouraged in that direction. An incorrect analysis of the phenomenon itself can give rise to inadequate policy prescriptions, whether for the government or for "civil society", to implement. It is relatively easy to identify two approaches in the literature on the basic processes of democratization and social progress in Indonesia, which can then impact on any analysis of decentralization.

One approach is represented by the "critical liberals" and "neo-marxists".[3] The scholars from these schools emphasize how decentralization has been accompanied by the domination in local politics of what Hadiz calls predatory elites.[4] However, as Aspinall explains, analysis by both the "neo-marxists" (as Hadiz is classified by Aspinall) and the "critical liberals", as Aspinall classifies himself, displays an "absence in their analysis of ... the transformative potential of subordinated groups". As a result of this absence, their works are only able to identify a key aspect of reality — the prevalence of the predatory elites — but then just throw up their hands about future prospects. Aspinall continues: both groups of scholars are "distinguished chiefly by their pessimism about the prospects of Indonesia's democratic transformation". This is indeed featured in Vedi Hadiz's *Localising Power in Post-Authoritarian Indonesia*, the major work to date on decentralization coming out of these perspectives. In Hadiz's book, the absence of any transformative power from the subordinated groups is formulated with reference to the state of the labour movement in Indonesia at the time of writing, but it is cursory and unserious, as is the treatment of the disorganization of civil society in the book he authored jointly with Richard Robison on the reorganization of power in the New Order.[5] Most of this analysis, including some with useful empirical data, simply concludes that decentralization is reinforcing predatory and corrupt practices and stops there. I will discuss Hadiz's comments on the labour movement in the final section of this essay.

The second perspective comes from scholars and also technocrats seeking policy prescription, usually within a framework using concepts such as "good governance". They are looking for an approach that can enhance what they see as the positive potential of decentralization policies. There is a commonsensical idea that some form of devolution in implementation responsibility seems natural for such a huge and geo-socially diverse country as Indonesia. In addition to that commonsensical orientation, much of the conceptual apparatus used by these scholars and technocrats comes from the Indonesian government's own conceptualization or from the large body of "good governance" literature, especially from donor agencies. Holtzappel and Ramstedt's book, *Decentralisation and Regional Autonomy in Indonesia*, is a good example of the research and analysis compiled by the World Bank, SMERU Research Institute, and Asia Foundation researchers as well as independent scholars working within the same framework. This technocratic approach is the main target of Hadiz's polemic in his book. He argues essentially that their approach is utopian in that it ignores the real conflicts between interests and attempts to impose prescriptions that have no power base. Hadiz is, I think, correct in this critique. Many of these scholars note the "many challenges from various interests that could divert the process from its ultimate goal",[6] referring to local economic and power interests. However, the solutions are not seen in *strategies related to changing the balance of power* but only in capacity building, as defined by skill sets.[7] Most of these scholars, including Holtzappel and Ramstedt, do attempt to offer prescriptions for improvement to what they generally acknowledge as a very flawed process. However, the weakness of their approach is manifested in that almost all of these prescriptions amount to urging more of the same, but just "better", i.e., better trained and improved administrative, managerial processes.

I will argue a perspective different from both of these. I am arguing that decentralization, in the specific form that has evolved since 2000, reflects two key features of Indonesian class structure and class politics. The first feature is that the power of crony capital has been greatly diminished. The political initiative from within the capitalist class has shifted to within the majority of the class, which comprises overwhelmingly local capital. This feature both explains the "rise of decentralization" as a policy prescription as well as the strength of local political intervention into national politics, most vividly represented by the rise of Joko Widodo. It also underpins the dysfunctional aspect of decentralization which is more or less dominated by initiatives from the local level, often of parochial character. There is not only increased tension between the local and the national, but also between districts or groups of districts. In the absence of a capitalist class with a strong national character, decentralization encourages a state of weak national coordination.

Second, the reorganization at a national level in parts of the non-capitalist classes (i.e., the mass of the formal and informal, rural and urban, proletariat) is still unfolding so that these classes are also only beginning to establish a national framework in which policies relating to social and political development can be developed. I will argue that decentralization is not producing a framework conducive to the formulation of policies which can address Indonesia's state of economic and social underdevelopment because there is not, as yet, any political agency based on organized social forces that is able to provide and impose a national framework.

While the technocratic approach poses the problem as one that can be solved by "capacity" building, Hadiz's approach poses no problem at all, except an intellectual problem of proving that the technocratic approach is flawed. Understanding the dysfunctional aspects of decentralization as a function of a lack in the national socio-political agency can direct us to an analysis which seeks to identify trends that might lead to providing such an agency and raises questions as to what policies might accelerate any such trends, or at least some of them. Here, however, I should emphasize that such policies may refer more to policies to be implemented by parts of "civil society", not so much policies to be implemented by the state. I will present an analysis in the final chapter of this essay pointing to two potential sources of initial national socio-political agency: the new trade union movement and the nationally aspiring elements within the local-level bourgeoisie, of whom Joko Widodo is a prime example.

First, however, it is necessary to review the origins of the contemporary version of *desentralisasi*.

Chapter I

The Enigmatic Emergence of Decentralization

During the last fourteen years (1999–2013), budgetary authority for spending a significant portion of the national revenue for activities to be carried out by the local apparatus of Indonesian national ministries has been delegated to sub-provincial governments and parliaments, that is town municipalities and county districts, known as *kabupaten*. At the moment, the core amount is provided through the General Allocation Fund (DAU) which is set at least 26 per cent of Net Domestic Revenue.[8] Regions with major natural resources that bring in foreign revenue also receive a percentage of those revenues, depending on the particular natural resource. There is also a provision for the special allocation of additional funds. This policy direction was also later strengthened by the introduction of direct elections for town mayors and county heads (*bupati*) as well as governors of provinces. The policies embodied in this new delegation of power, legalized by a series of laws after 2000, are known as the *desentralisasi* policies.[9]

There can be little doubt that among Indonesian political scientists, and the few Indonesia specialists outside the country, *desentralisasi* has been one of the most written-about topics in recent scholarly literature on Indonesian politics. There is a plethora of Indonesian honours, masters and doctoral theses on this topic. In realpolitik terms, *desentralisasi* in and of itself has

not brought about major changes in Indonesian politics. The
policy has not brought about a change in direction, in terms of
either economic or social strategy nor changed — as yet — the
underlying character, outlook and activity of those who wield
power in Indonesia or their subjects. However, as I have stated
earlier, there is also no doubt that the coming of *desentralisasi*
is a *result* of two colossal changes in both the political and
economic format of Indonesia: the end of authoritarian rule and
of Suhartoist crony capitalism.

Reformasi and the Absence of *Desentralisasi*

Perhaps the best starting point for an analysis of the phenomenon
of *desentralisasi* in Indonesia over the last decade is to note that
advocacy for decentralization was completely absent within
the movement against authoritarian rule that developed in the
1990s. While I will argue that in its current form, it is a result of
the end of authoritarian rule, it was not a result intended by the
forces that composed the pro-democracy movement. In fact, it
is hard to find a single demand for decentralization mentioned
anywhere in the political statements and manifestos in any of the
important elements from the anti-dictatorship movement of the
1990s. Despite the escalating criticism on the concentration of
power, even of *sentralistik* (centralistic) power, the reality is that
nobody among the active political forces arraigned against Suharto
formulated an opposing perspective to advocate decentralization
as part of an alternative programme. The overall rhetoric
countering centralization of power only advocated democracy,
not decentralization or federalism.

Yet within two years of Suharto's downfall, a full-scale
decentralization was underway, moving faster than almost any
other medium-term reform being considered. Furthermore,

within four to five years, the initial reforms were deepened with the introduction of direct elections for *bupati* and mayors. The political significance of this anomaly cannot be underestimated. It poses two crucial questions: why was it not high on the anti-authoritarian movement's agenda; and then, where did the push for these policies come from? It is especially the second question that may open the way to understanding what changes in Indonesia decentralization actually represents.

It is worth reminding the reader with some representative examples of the kind of advocacy that was happening during the 1990s, noting the emphasis on democracy and anti-authoritarianism and opposition to corruption, and the absence of any mention of decentralization.

Certainly by the mid-1990s, around 1996, the movement had formulated and established some central demands. These demands came out of the activist backbone of the movement and represented an agenda won by their persistent propaganda and their obvious aptness in terms of the situation and aspirations of the urban poor, working class and lower middle classes whom they mobilized on the streets, or whose aspirations they politicized in other ways. Through hundreds of bulletins, newsletters, pamphlets, press statements, placards and posters, and the actions they used to build and magnify a clear series of demands that evolved were later adopted almost unanimously. The primary demands were:

1. repeal *dwifungsi* ABRI (end the dual function of the armed forces);
2. repeal the laws that controlled party and electoral life;
3. end corruption, collusion and nepotism;
4. force Suharto out; and
5. reduce prices or increase wages.

Whether in statements by the activist wing of the anti-dictatorship movement or comments from the more "loyal opposition" wing (Amien Rais, Megawati Sukarnoputri, for example) it is almost impossible to find advocacy of decentralization before 1998–99.

A typical summary on the demands of the activist wing from the anti-Suharto movement can be found in the statement issued by the National Committee for Democratic Struggle (KNPD) in January 1998.[10]

- A succession and democratic mechanisms to elect a new president and vice-president.
- An investigation into the wealth of government officials and their families.
- The withdrawal of the five repressive political laws.
- A change in the system of government to make it possible for the political parties to enter the cabinet.
- Wipe out corruption, collusion and the conglomerates, towards an economic system which is clean and for the people.
- Reduce the social and political role of the armed forces and the abolition of the Dual Function of the armed forces. The military's social and political role be carried out through a military representative in the MPR [Majelis Permusyawaratan Rakyat, or People's Consultative Assembly] in a composition that is just and proportional.
- A reduction in prices of essential items.
- Upholding the basic principles of human rights in accordance with the Universal Declaration of Human Rights.

Another set of demands came from a more moderate activist formation, PIJAR:[11]

- A reduction in prices and stabilization of the rupiah.
- A complete overhaul of the cabinet.
- A new president.

These two sets of demands captured the spirit and scope of the overwhelming majority of forces mobilizing during the 1990s against the regime. In the latter part of the development of the movement against Suharto, figures who were previously supportive or at least acquiescent became more vocal. In 1997, after the parliamentary elections, Amien Rais, then Chairperson of Muhammadiyah and a leading personality in Ikatan Cendikiawan Muslim Indonesia (ICMI), which was headed by Suharto himself, also became very outspoken. Although mostly initially formulating proposed reforms in abstract terms, he made it very clear he was for a change of presidency. While Rais later played an important role in paving the way for *desentralisasi*, he gave no inkling of such a demand between 1997 and 1998 when he latched on to the anti-Suharto movement. For example, Amien Rais in early 1998 explains:

> There are some agendas that are always stored in my head. First, all of the natural wealth, whether in the forests or mountains or in the belly of the earth, such as minerals, has to be saved for our grandchildren. I am sure now that there is a fatal mismanagement of our tropical forests as well as minerals, oil and gas as well as others. Second, there has to be the stage-by-stage establishment of clean government, by handling two chronic problems, corruption and collusions. Third, there must be optimal efforts to reduce the widening gap between the haves and the have-nots. This gap hast to be reduced systematically and by stages. Fourth, *Bhinneka Tunggal Ika* [Unity in Diversity] must be defended totally and must not be allowed to be touched in

any way at all. Any attempt to question this will put Indonesia as
a nation and country in danger. Fifth, there needs to be a grand
alliance between ABRI (TNI AD) [Armed Forces – Army], Golkar
[Golongan Karya], the parties, mass organizations, universities,
business, NGOs and others which have not yet been too touched
by the pollution of corruption and collusion. It is hoped that
this grand and clean coalition will take on the national tasks
of the future. Reform measures will need to be implemented
step-by-step so that nobody is startled. Radical and dramatic
policies will only worsen the situation.[12]

He made no mention of decentralization or any related issue.

Megawati Sukarnoputri began to emerge as a symbol of
anti-Suhartoism in 1991, but more as a result of her stubborn
resistance to the Suharto government's efforts to remove her from
the leadership of one of the officially sanctioned parties, the PDI
(Indonesian Democratic Party). Later she also espoused a reform
agenda of sorts. In the same report cited above when Rais spoke,
Megawati also presented her vision:

We have to create a clean and authoritative government:
1. A government that can decide policies in accordance with
   the Peoples Mandate of Suffering;
2. A government whose officials are not involved in business
   through collusion, corruption and nepotism;
3. A government that can be and is willing to be controlled by law
   and the people via democratic and judicial institutions.[13]

Again there was no hint of a mention on decentralization or
any related issue.

Nowhere in any of the political statements of the activist
coalitions or from the "loyal opposition" figures did the advocacy
of decentralization receive any significant mention. What advocacy

there was for decentralization before 1998 did not come from the movement against Suharto but from within technocratic circles, outside, or at best, on the outer margins of the opposition.[14] For example, in the same report cited above, Emil Salim, a former technocratic minister in the Suharto cabinet, advocates "*desentralisasi pembangunan*" (developmental decentralization). However, figures such as these played no role in advancing the movement against authoritarian rule nor added any colour or content to the demands of that movement.

Activists and participants in the protest and opposition movement that escalated during the 1990s often used the word "*sentralistik*" to critique the New Order regime as having centralized power in the hands of a small clique or a single family. But there was almost never a formulation of a solution to this centralism as decentralization. This, of course, makes clear sense as the centralization that was being talked about as *sentralistik* was not being either defined by geography or administrative layers (national versus district) but rather in terms of personalities or political factions. Furthermore, until late 1997, the two main political vehicles for the opposition, the People's Democratic Party (PRD) intersecting with the activist wing of the opposition on the one hand and the more moderate Megawati Sukarnoputri's PDI were both organizations which had strong national, and in Megawati's case, nationalistic, perspectives. Megawati also inherited the pre-1965 hostility to federalism (connected to its early sponsorship in the 1940s by Dutch colonialism).

The fact that it was the PRD and other activist groups and the Megawati PDI that were the key vehicles for opposition also emphasizes that the social composition of the backbone of the opposition were sections of society that had been alienated from the state and its apparatus. Neither the student nor worker–urban poor base that the activists were appealing to nor the small

business and regional urban poor (in specific regions) base of the
PDI (from 1996 the PDI-P) held a serious number of senior state
apparatus positions anywhere, including at the district level. Local
state apparatus were in the hands of a bureaucratic caste that had
been integrated into a centralized state apparatus and which had
no material base that might inspire ambitions to campaign for a
delegation of power over budget in a decentralized direction.

Their integration into the machine had been reflected in
May 1997, only a year before the fall of Suharto, when the state
machinery located in the villages, towns and *kabupaten* was able
to organize elections where Suharto's party scored its highest
ever victory.[15] The integration of local state machinery into a
centralized state machine which denied other possibilities of
formal power bases is well described by Sidel:

> During the three decades of the Soeharto era (1966–1998), the
> Indonesian state was tightly centralized and insulated from
> centrifugal and societal constraints on the internal circulation
> and machinations of its officials. Although pseudo-parliamentary
> bodies at the district, provincial, and national levels were
> regularly elected on a five-year cycle, their effective powers and
> prerogatives were severely limited. Electoral competition was
> confined to three parties, Golkar, the United Development Party
> (PPP), and the Indonesian Democratic Party (PDI), with Golkar
> enjoying tremendous advantages — and persistent majorities
> — as the government's political machine, and PPP and PDI
> restricted to minor supporting roles. At the district and provincial
> levels, local executives were essentially imposed by the Ministry
> of Internal Affairs and vested with powers that dwarfed those
> of the elected assemblies, while at the national level a supra-
> parliamentary body stacked with carefully selected appointees
> convened on a quinquennial basis to re-elect Soeharto and his
> anointed vice-president. A multi-tiered hierarchy of military

commands mirrored the structure of local government, and active and retired officers were appointed not only to reserved seats in the regional assemblies and the national parliament but also to nearly half the governorships and regencies in the country. Active and retired military officers staffed countless other local and national government positions and, at least until the 1990s, dominated the leadership of Golkar, which operated as a centralized and "closed-list" dominant party throughout the New Order.

The implications of this organization of state power were obvious: the possibilities for the emergence of "local strongmen" were highly restricted. Officials at all levels of the state hierarchy were highly responsive to demands and directives from "above", as their assignments and promotions depended entirely on appointments determined in Jakarta.[16]

The anti-dictatorship movement had no base inside this apparatus. And there were no elements of this apparatus with an independent base that might have wanted to ally with the opposition to seek more power through advocating decentralization, i.e., delegation of budgetary power from the national to local governments.

Desentralisasi was not a demand of the "constituency" that comprised the anti-dictatorship movement, neither in its radical nor moderate manifestations. The emergence of the advocacy for decentralization came after the fall of Suharto as a new constituency ascended. An initial early spokesperson for one version of decentralization, "federalism", did emerge from among the moderate latecomers to the anti-dictatorship movement, namely Amien Rais. However, he did not seriously campaign for a federalist reform orientation until late 1998 and then the PDI-P-Megawati forces strongly opposed his orientation. It was not an important feature of Rais's statements from before May

1998. Support for a federal state was part of the programme of the National Mandate Party (PAN) since its foundation in late 1998. Rais was its first chairperson.

Where Did *Desentralisasi* Come From?

The movement and advocacy for change that evolved during the 1990s proved adequate to dislodge a thirty-three-year-old dictatorship, protected by the Armed Forces. This power was adequate therefore also to force through some other key changes in the immediate aftermath of Suharto's fall. These changes included a steady process of removing the Armed Forces from its repressive political role (except in Papua and Aceh) and from Parliament. All of the laws containing restrictions on political parties were lifted. The election laws of 1999 withdrew all existing restrictions, except the ban on spreading Marxism-Leninism. The 1999 elections operated under almost no repressive conditions — although major elite elements were able to claw back their privilege later. Cronyism and nepotism suffered an immediate major blow simply by the removal of an authoritarian ruler who wielded centralized power — Suharto was the lynchpin of cronyism during the New Order. Of course, in all of these areas over the last ten years there have been clawbacks. But the power of the movement at the time was very impressive. In some areas, the legislative clawback has been ineffective, such as in the labour arena. President Habibie very quickly ended state control of trade unions in 1998. Ten years later, there was a significant beginning to a new trade union movement.

It was also Habibie who moved quickly to prepare the legislation that brought in decentralization. He asked technocrat Ryaas Rasyid to form a group (Tim Tujuh) to formulate policy and legislation. In fact, the thinking that some kind of decentralization was needed in Indonesia had long developed within the Suharto government, among regime leaders, the technocracy and the military. The MPR Decision No. 15 in 1998 had already foreshadowed consideration of looking for ways to grant more autonomy at the district level.[17]

Bureaucrats and technocrats within the New Order state apparatus were confronted simply with the increasing complexity of on the ground policy implementation given Indonesia's size (always growing in population, and so far in GDP), its island structure and socio-ethnic configuration. The structures of government administration needed some way to deal with policy implementation and the ability to deal with smaller administrative units with more flexibility based on differing local conditions. The main thing holding them back from moving in this direction was the fear that it would encourage a federalist dynamic, a more "radical and dramatic" devolution of real power. The regime was interested in improving the implementation of its policies through decentralization, making them more specific to local conditions, not in delegating too much real power as would be the case in a federal system. There was also, among some, fears of federalism encouraging secessionism. Rasyid himself had made this concern clear many times. He spoke at the Australian National University "Indonesia Update 2002" which was funded by the Australian Ministry of Foreign Affairs and attended by academics and bureaucrats:

> Any attempt to shift power to the provinces would have been read by the conservative Unitarians as promoting federalism, by extension placing at risk national coherence and integrity. Inevitably this would have ignited a bitter public debate. The Habibie government had maintained from its inception that the period of extreme centralism was over, but that it did not want to be labeled federalist. The focus of regional authority was therefore on the district and municipality (*kabupaten/kota*) rather than provincial level of government.[18]

Rasyid, who also served as a cabinet minister in the later Abdurrahman Wahid government until he resigned, echoed the common sense style formulations often found within the technocracy:

> The policy was intended to provide more scope for local creativity and initiative in making policy and promoting public participation.[19]

The fear of being labelled federalist or of unleashing a federalist dynamic was no doubt also underpinned by the semi-federal system of representation that Indonesia has long possessed. Indonesia's formal structures of representation and government have long been highly contradictory. The formal representative system comprises national, provincial, *kabupaten* and municipal-elected parliaments. The structure of government, however, has been based on national ministries who implement policies at the local level through local offices of the national ministries. Governors and *bupati*s were essentially officials within the national governmental structure appointed by the national government, after it had considered recommendations and votes in the local parliaments. The existence of these provincial and local parliaments was "natural" given Indonesia's socio-geographical reality: its diversity and unevenness on the one hand and its huge size on the other. They were also a political infrastructure potentially able to facilitate any federalist dynamics that might be unleashed. And the reality of a non-industrializing capitalism, where small and medium local businesses operating only at the local level servicing small local markets comprised the vast majority of the capitalist elite, meant that a federal dynamic could not be ruled out. Decentralization was on the agenda *within* the New Order regime, but the New Order had not yet, by May 1998, been able to find a way to implement it, being afraid of the federalist dynamic.

Almost all the literature on *desentralisasi* associates it with democratization and *reformasi*. However, the reality is that the first push after May 1998 in this direction came from within the government, not from the pro-democracy movement. As demonstrated earlier, decentralization never figured in any of the demands of that movement.

There were forces which did always tend towards defending a centralistic approach that exercised influence during the Habibie interregnum: the Armed Forces and the largest cronies themselves. However, while still influential, these two power centres had suffered major blows. The May 1998 uprising delivered a major blow to the prestige of the Armed Forces. Its primary political role since at least 1965 had been to underpin the political rule of General Suharto. When Suharto resigned and was followed by General Wiranto, as head of the Armed Forces, announcing that the Army would protect Suharto as an individual, it was an admission that the Army had failed in this fundamental role. This was despite a hardening of repressive actions from around June 1996, including the beginning of killings and disappearances. The triumph of the unarmed, anti-dictatorship protest movement over Suharto, despite Army backing, not only ended authoritarian rule, but also weakened the influence of the Army.[20] The Army suffered another major blow when it was unable to deliver the success it had promised the ruling elite on the occasion of the referendum on independence in East Timor later in September 1999.

The end of dictatorial rule meant increased room for political activity for those who had been mobilized to oppose the New

Order, workers, urban poor and students. President Habibie also quickly moved to ratify the International Labour Organization (ILO) conventions guaranteeing trade union rights. Most political prisoners were released.

At the same time that these sectors won more democratic space, the few scores of big business conglomerates that had been protected by the military-backed ruling Suharto faction lost the special protection of their privileged position that they had previously enjoyed. These were the major components of what had been called crony capitalism. The biggest cronies were the Suharto children and relatives, but there were several others as well. With the end of Suharto's authoritarian rule, *all these ceased to be cronies.* Cronies are not simply big capital with close links to state power: all capitalists are, in the end, close to state power in a capitalist society. Cronies are made up of individual big capitalists who are especially protected and coddled by the state, including in their relationships with other capitalists. *The fall of Suharto and the blows delivered to the Army ended this specific format of capitalism — crony capitalism.* It will be argued below that the end of crony capitalism is deeply connected to the momentum for decentralization. The cronies, previously protected by a military-backed national level ruling clique, now face other capitalists in a competition for power where winning popularity becomes important.

These two centralistic power centres — the Army and the cronies — had been weakened and had lost their monopoly over political initiative, but they still hovered ready to reassert their leadership. Habibie assessed that it was not wise to prevaricate on this issue.[21] He commissioned Rasyid to draft the legislation and shepherded it quickly through the Parliament, even before the early elections held in 1999. This initiative was supported by the mainly ideologically driven foreign "donor" technocracy.

Habibie as a Technocratic Interregnum

There is some literature that tends to look at the introduction of decentralization as an attempt by technocratic forces to impose a "good governance" formula on Indonesia. The most substantial of these is Vedi Hadiz's *Localising Power in Post-Authoritarian Indonesia* where Hadiz argues that this technocratic imposition was bound to fail in the face of the reality that decentralization was essentially the location of a conflict of interests, mainly what he calls "predatory" local elites. Hadiz's book, while sometimes asserting itself as political economy, lacks any fundamental analysis of national class politics and thus is unable to present a framework for understanding the process he is focusing on. Of course, he is correct at one level of empirical description, namely that local business elites are the main beneficiaries of this policy. However, he fails to fill out the picture to make it clear why large national level capital has not been a player, and, in conjunction with this, fails also to provide the context for the technocratic push that took place when Habibie commissioned the drafting of decentralization legislation.

Habibie's brief presidency was an interregnum, brought about as a consequence of the Suhartoist faction members sacrificing Suharto and its monopoly power as a concession to the mass discontent on the streets. These protests were immediately threatening a state of ungovernability as well as held the potential to deepen and radicalize the protest movement. Suharto, as well as his and their monopoly on power, was given up to save the system. The task to manage the transition fell on Vice-President Habibie who was sworn in as president. While Habibie was a favourite of Suharto, he was not a major power in the faction. He had never held a ministry with political clout, nor control over the central lever of the economy. He had been able to develop his own business group, but it was on the fringes compared to the Suharto family or any of the big, core cronies that controlled huge conglomerates, and even media. He was not a Bob Hasan, Aburizal Bakrie, or Surya Paloh. In fact, Habibie was the technocratic fig leaf to Suharto's crony capitalism. He was the man who ran ICMI, the highest profile association of intellectuals and technocrats in the country. His own little fiefdom had been over scientific and technological research, both via ministerial positions as well as his control over one of Indonesia's state-owned aircraft production companies. Even this, however, was not core to Suharto's actual (very late) attempts to encourage real industrialization which Suharto did by assisting Texmaco industrialist, Marimutu Srinavasan.[22]

The 1960s and 1970s Berkeley Mafia technocrats had been edged out as a hindrance to crony capitalism, which had an opportunistic and pragmatic orientation to many economic decisions. The later technocracy, represented by Habibie, was essentially ornamental. However, this dramatically changed, even if only briefly, with Suharto's resignation and the end of the monopoly on (military-backed) power by his faction. The cronies, also weakened by the devastation of the Asian financial crisis, no longer held the initiative. The highly crony-dominated Suharto cabinet gave way to Habibie's which, while still using many Suharto cabinet members, began a shift to the technocracy. Symbolic of the beginning to this shift was the removal of the head of the Bank of Indonesia from the cabinet, making it more independent. More technocrats were brought on board as advisors in various capacities, including in relation to decentralization. One of his advisors, Dewi Fortuna Anwar, explained the advisors' influential role on this issue:

> The task of drafting the bills was given to a group of academics
> from the Institute for Government Studies (Institut Ilmu

Pemerintahan, IIP) under Professor Ryaas Rasyid, a well-known specialist on local government. Although the political climate at the time was strongly in favour of regional autonomy, the drafters and many members of the cabinet insisted that autonomy should only be given to the second tier of government, the district/mayoralty level. Ostensibly this was to bring government and public services closer to the people; but the real reason was based on fear that giving autonomy to the provinces, which were larger and stronger administrative units, would lead to federalism.[23]

The collapse of crony and military factional power, in the face of mass protests, had facilitated the installation of a man who had, up until May 1998, played a primarily symbolic role: the technocratic and intellectual face of the regime. During his presidency, as Dewi Fortuna Anwar also correctly explains, Habibie facilitated changes consistent with technocratic formulations of how a liberal democratic government might operate.

This technocracy, based in some sections of the civil service as well as the universities and research institutions, had also evolved separately from crony capitalism. These people, such as Ryaas Rasyid, were either bearers of the original New Order rhetoric on development, which they took seriously or of the tradition of criticism of New Order development strategy, represented by journals such as *Prisma* or others, which were oriented to the priority of supporting local-level development. Intellectuals at Gadjah Mada University, such as Professor Pratikno, had also been advocating decentralization as a means to enliven local decision making.[24] They were both groups of people who had been sidelined under crony capitalism and were eager to reassert technocratic norms. Many worked with their like-minded technocrats among donor aid agencies. The Habibie interregnum opened up a chance for them to intervene. This was possible only because of the unexpected success of the mass anti-dictatorship movement in ending crony capitalist dictatorial rule.[25]

The technocratic interregnum was accidental in the sense that the technocratic token of Habibie had been appointed to the powerless position of vice-president with no real consideration that he would end up a president. It was the fact of the collapse of the dictatorship under pressure from below rather than as a result of an internally managed succession that meant that the Suharto faction was not in a position to determine succession appropriate to the survival of cronyism. Furthermore, this technocratic initiative was strongly supported by the "donor" technocracy. While a full picture of donor intervention is not clear from available studies, it does seem that the Asian Development Bank (ADB) played a major role.

The Indonesian government had approached the ADB as early as 1998 to assist with planning decentralization. The ADB responded with a Community and Local Government Support (CLGS) programme, supplemented with four Technical Assistance packages all aimed at promoting decentralization. Over the next few years, the ADB's programme expanded further based on a 2001 Country Operational Strategy Study (COSS) followed by a 2002 Country Strategy and Program (CSP) for 2003–05 and then a further one for 2006–09. The components of ADB intervention supporting decentralization appear to involve expenditures above US$15 million. The programmes covered several major ministries and areas of service delivery, transportation and urban planning.[26]

The synergy with foreign donor technocracy — which needs further documentation — no doubt gave the technocratic interregnum additional strength, and the whole decentralization process technical back-up (even if only partially effective) as well as an additional layer of legitimacy.

Federalism?

Once the dictatorship had been removed, however, a pro-federal dynamic outside the Habibie government did develop very quickly, although not from the activist section of the pro-democracy movement. This was separate from the government's push towards decentralization laws. The main advocate for a federal system, i.e. a delegation of real powers in some areas to provinces, was Amien Rais. Rais was a central leader of the Indonesian Muslim Intellectual Association (ICMI), headed by Suharto and managed by Habibie. As head of the Muhammadiyah in 1997, he was the lone religious leader who did not join a call by religious leaders to boycott the 1997 elections. After those elections however, he turned dissident.

The New Order political leadership and state apparatus had stalled on decentralizing, afraid of any tendency towards federalism. It was Amien Rais who most seriously raised the banner of federalism, almost immediately after Suharto's fall. Federalism became a formal part of the platform of the party, the Partai Amanat Nasional (PAN), which Rais helped form early in 1999 for the elections that year.[27] Rais's clear advocacy of a federal state was part of his electoral positioning for the 1999 parliamentary elections, and the MPR presidential electoral process which would follow. Rais was explicit in his demands and argumentation at the time. He argued in October 1999, for example:

> A federal state is needed in order to overcome several fundamental problems, that is, imbalances in the social, economic, political and cultural fields. A federal state perspective is needed in order to restore human rights and to develop a balance between centre and regions.
>
> ...
>
> Revenue sharing between centre and region are unbalanced.

Regions enjoy too little from their natural resources. The central government with its corruption, collusion and nepotism (KKN) gets too much of these revenues.[28]

From at least this time onwards, he campaigned with this argument. In November, he argued again:

First, retaining the unitary state, with its extraordinary concentration of power on Jakarta will grow exploitation outside Java by Jakarta and give rise to KKN everywhere. "Enough, we must say goodbye to this," he affirmed, stating that forcing itself to retain a unitary state will lead to Indonesia's collapse ...[29]

He added:

The next option is a federal system — an option that is a "golden road" to satisfy the regions' discontent.

The campaign created a major national resonance such that in 1999 even a politician like Golkar's Akbar Tandjung was willing to contemplate, even if briefly, a nationwide referendum on the issue:

A referendum whose spirit is to offer options of a federal system or greatest possible autonomy would have to be carried out nationally as it affects the form of the state.[30]

Rais's campaign took place at a time when "separatist" sentiment was also high on the political agenda. There was increasing activity supporting independence in both Papua and Aceh. While dissent, resistance and repression in Papua were, and still are, long-term issues which have been, to a certain extent, accommodated into the Indonesian political elite's consciousness as an ongoing problem that can be lived with, the rise in protest activity in Aceh was a different matter. The movement for a referendum grew loudly all during 1999, peaking in a massive rally of hundreds of thousands demanding a referendum in November 1999. This helped form a climate in which Rais's campaign for a federal state appeared to have some basis. Perhaps even more significant than the rising clamour for a referendum in Aceh, were the calls for a federal state, or even independence, from another resource rich region of Indonesia, East Kalimantan.

The extent of East Kalimantan's resource base was already clear in 1999. It was, and is, one of the most endowed regions of Indonesia: oil, gas, coal, gold and land suitable for palm oil. What is special about the federal call from East Kalimantan, unlike the calls for separatism from Aceh and Papua, is that it came from an area where there was no basis for claims of national or ethnic repression. The political and business elite of East Kalimantan, who were advocating a federal state, is multi-ethnic with key elements of the elite coming from outside Kalimantan: from Sulawesi and Java, as well as from ethnic groups based in Borneo. The East Kalimantan elite "identity", such as it is, is being formed not based on ethnicity, culture or shared political repression, but rather out of an acquisitive orientation to natural resources.

The East Kalimantan elite, through the East Kalimantan provincial parliament, on 8 November 1999 passed a resolution supporting Rais's call. However, the parliament divided along party lines. The PDI-P, Golkar, and parties that had come out of Golkar opposed the support for a federal Indonesia. The other parties, mostly connected to Islamic politics, including Rais's party, supported the federal state idea. However — and this is crucial for future developments — both pro- and anti-federalist parties demanded a massive increase in the proportion of the revenue generated out of East Kalimantan's resource sector that should stay in Kalimantan. The regional parliament's resolution demanded 75 per cent of revenues remain in East Kalimantan.[31] The demands for a federal state even had echoes in calls for independence from some parts of the East Kalimantan elite.

The crucial thing to note here is that this federalist, even separatist call, stems from a purely financial sense of "oppression" by an avaricious elite. Similar calls came from parts of East Nusa Tenggara and also from Riau.[32] The support for a federal state came from the local political and business elites in natural resource-rich regions. The "national" political parties that supported Rais's federal state were, of course, his own — PAN — and other Islamic parties. All these parties' leaderships are based within the elite formations of local areas, mostly off the island of Java.

The federal idea lost out in the ensuing manoeuvring. Rais's advocacy climaxed during the presidency of Abdurrahman Wahid, while Rais was still chairperson of the MPR. At that time the Armed Forces still had formal representation in the parliament and also argued against a federal state, reviving the term "Negara Kesatuan Republik Indonesia". PDI-P and Golkar also resisted, as did President Wahid. However, out of this campaign came a consolidation of the acceptance of the compromise embodied in Habibie's 1999 legislation, responding primarily to the real motor behind the calls for a federal state, namely "fiscal repression". Even in Aceh and Papua, while the driving force was the military oppression and discrimination against the local population, their calls for independence were also accompanied by justifications demanding more revenue for the regions from natural resource based income, usually articulated to appeal to all classes.

The discussion earlier on Amien Rais's advocacy of federalism and the calls from local elites for a federal system from areas such as East Kalimantan, for referendums in Aceh and West Papua and for various degrees of decentralization even from within Java,[33] all indicate that the technocratic interregnum's push on decentralization was happening in a conducive atmosphere. The most concrete manifestation of this, in Java as well as on other islands, has been the massive increase of new *kabupaten* — around 200 — and some new provinces. It quickly garnered support from that huge section of the capitalist class — local capital — that had hitherto been overshadowed by the big, crony conglomerates.

Consolidation of *Desentralisasi*

The federal idea was defeated but in the process *desentralisasi* has been consolidated. All of the laws formalizing decentralization have been implemented without serious impediment.

Also consolidating this new system were the amendments to the Indonesian Constitution between 1999 and 2002 which specifically address the appeals for more regional autonomy. Most importantly, these established the Regional Representative Council (DPD). The DPD comprises members elected to represent the regions, with equal representation from each region. These members are also members of the Peoples' Consultative Assembly (MPR) replacing those MPR members that were appointed by the president under the old system. The official summary of the amendments states:

> It [the DPD] has the freedom to further the general interest of the regions vis-à-vis the government and to submit to the national parliament proposals for new statutes and amendments of statutes that concern the subject of regional autonomy in its broadest sense. Its membership consists of delegates from the regions, which in this case means the provinces.[34]

By 2002, the Constitution had been amended to legitimize a general change in stance on the regions:

> Regional Government has broad autonomy, with the understanding that the regional share in the exploitation of natural resources as stipulated by the respective law and regulation will be used to raise the region's progress and prosperity. Regional autonomy including the servicing of the local communities has to be executed and remains within the authority of the unitary state of the Republic of Indonesia. The newly amended constitution also refers the state's recognition of, and respect for, regional administration units which are special or extraordinary in character to statute.[35]

Embedded constitutionally by 2002, the new system has not been challenged in any serious way. One manifestation of the consolidation of *desentralisasi* by 2013 has been the increased profile and national political weight of directly elected governors, *bupati* and mayors. The rise to national prominence of Joko Widodo is just one example. Another example is Deputy Governor of Jakarta, Basuki Tjahaja Purnama, also known by his nickname Ahok, who first won national prominence as *bupati* of Belitung Timur off Sumatra. Other local political figures such as Tri Rismaharini, mayor of Surabaya as well as Ganjar Pranowo, elected as Governor of Central Java in 2013, are also increasingly spoken of as potential national political leaders. The emergence of political figures onto the national stage via local positions is itself consolidating the whole system of regional autonomy. These positions become platforms as the devolved financial power and authority over programmes aimed at regional "progress and prosperity" provide scope for the people in these positions to be identified with the delivery of services, whether real or illusionary. The "Fiscal Balance" law has been guaranteeing at least 26 per

cent of Net Domestic Revenue to local governments during an
eight year period of massively increasing revenues — at least 400
per cent. In regions which have also received payments under
the resource originating revenue sharing laws, there have been
up to and even over 1,000 per cent increases in revenues for
local government, such as that experienced by East Kalimantan
over the last ten years.

There has been some opposition to one aspect of the system
from the post pro-authoritarian wing of Indonesian politics via
presidential hopeful, former Lieutenant General Prabowo. He has
argued for an end to the direct election of the *bupati*, mayor and
governor positions:

> The direct regional elections for *bupati* and governor should be
> re-thought together, whether it is too much of a luxury for the
> nation ... I think the direct elections for governor and *bupati*
> should be re-thought, may be keep the open vote in the DPRD
> [regional parliament], so that elected DPRD members vote and
> the electors can see who their representatives voted for.[36]

However, these calls have received little support. All of the existing
parties have now integrated themselves into a political rhythm
based on the direct elections of governors, *bupati* and mayors.
There is no challenge to this; in fact, the rise in profile of regional
leaders is reinforcing this new local-national balance.

Chapter II

The Political Economy of *Desentralisasi*

A primary thesis of this essay is that the sudden emergence of decentralization, seemingly out of nowhere (but actually initiated from within the technocracy) and its strong consolidation over the last ten years is a direct consequence of two interlinked phenomenon. Firstly, the end of crony capitalism. And secondly, in some ways more fundamentally, that Indonesia's general economic underdevelopment has not fostered the growth of a large, strong national capitalist class, i.e., a class with a strong presence throughout the country with a concomitant national perspective, even if one emphasizing its own interests. The inability of Indonesia to industrialize over the last fifty years has meant that most capitalists in Indonesia are small, local capitalists, orienting to limited local markets. The larger capitalists have either evolved as protected cronies, or in very specific market niches, which give limited political clout. And, for a country the size of Indonesia, this group is not only not made up of industrialists, but also small in number.

Conglomerate, Crony vis-à-vis Local Capital

Indonesia has a population of 240 million people, 80 per cent of the United States' population size. It is likely that by 2050

Indonesia will have overtaken the population size of the United States. It is predicted to reach 450 million. Their gross domestic products (GDP) are, of course, very different from each other. The U.S. GDP for 2012–13 is US$15.7 trillion.[37] Indonesia's GDP is just under US$900 billion. The U.S. per capita income for 2012–13 is close to US$50,000 whereas Indonesia's is US$3,500.[38] It is not surprising that in economies which are so hugely different in scale, their capitalist classes are also very different in scale and nature. This class, to the extent it assumes the role of ruling class, may "rule" over a smaller economy than that of the United States but politically it has to manage a huge and complex country of 250 million people, heading to 450 million, with an island geography and massive issues of underdevelopment.

One way to get a picture of this is to compare the number of billionaires in each economy and also the nature of their enterprises. According to the *Forbes* listing, the United States has 442 billionaires to Indonesia's 25 billionaires. The majority of the Indonesian billionaires are listed by *Forbes* as being worth less than US$2 billion. A perusal of the interests of the Indonesian billionaires also indicates the extent to which their enterprises are not based on industrialization. *Forbes* lists only three as active in manufacturing: in tobacco, polyester and palm oil. It also lists one tyre manufacturer and one active in heavy equipment. *Forbes* lists only one investments billionaire. The single biggest group of 6 billionaires are coal exporters. Even if we take the list beyond these 25 billionaires to the richest 150 capitalists in Indonesia, the profile will not change much.

In June 2013, *Asia Globe* published a comprehensive summary description of the richest 150 Indonesians. Their net worth ranged from US$15.5 billion to US$93 million. Of these 150, 109 are listed of having a net worth under US$1 billion. *Asia Globe* lists 41 millionaires. Over 40 are assessed at being worth US$300 million or less. A perusal of the listing of the 150 shows very quickly that very few are involved in heavy industry, steel or even manufacturing. Even when they are, they are usually in the section of the list of capitalists worth US$200 million or less or where manufacturing is not a key component.

Only two companies are listed as being involved in steel manufacturing, and they are relatively small. Most of what is listed as manufacturing is mere assembly, as in electronics, automobiles and garments. None are involved in any serious way with the manufacture of plant and machinery. Low-cost consumer items, such as cigarettes, sanitary wear, food products and plastic goods, dominate. The only product with a relatively high unit price that Indonesian produces is automobiles. Here too the emphasis is on assembly of mostly (though not entirely) imported components. The profile of the 150 companies, heavy on banking, property, retail, coal and palm oil, is very much a hodgepodge, reflecting the ad hoc, state-protected, opportunistic evolution of Indonesian capitalism. Very few of the big companies deal with a genuinely national market, and where they do so only as retailers of light manufacturing products.

In November 2000, the United Nations Industrial Development Organisation (UNIDO) completed a detailed study of the Indonesian economy. The picture of very shallow "industrialization" painted then still applies today.

> While the government assiduously promoted export-oriented industrialization since 1985, neither the government nor the private sector accompany this drive with the necessary measures to diversify export products and markets, to deepen and diversify the manufacturing base, and to enhance the competitiveness of Indonesian firms. The absence of these measures to compensate for known market failures in building up manufacturing capability such as inadequate information, high risks and long and expensive learning process (Lall 1993 and Lall 1995), and the sheer rapidity of industrialization, led

to a relatively shallow industrial structure, while the promised foreign exchange earnings failed to materialize.

A number of other structural problems emerged. The oil and gas sector generated only limited net revenues. Low productivity plagued the small and medium-scale industries, while significant market concentration by a few large firms prevailed in large segments of manufacturing. Manufacturing production remained concentrated in Java, and in Greater Jakarta in particular. The capacity to absorb, adapt and developing process and product technology as well as human resources remained weak.[39]

The UNIDO report analyses the industrial depth of manufacturing and the nature of the technologies being deployed.

The pattern of Indonesian industrialization differed from that of other countries with similar degrees of industrialization. Between 1985 and 1997, the contribution of higher technology industries to manufacturing value-added did not increase, while the production of low-technology industries expanded, mainly at the expense of medium-technology industries. The increase in the share of low technology industries was due to the rapid growth of labour-intensive industries such as textiles, garments and footwear, and to a lesser extent to the expansion of the resource-based food, paper and wood industries. In contrast to the decline of the share of medium-technology industries in Indonesia (including rubber and plastic industries, fertilizer, cement, basic metals and simple fabricated metal industry), virtually all countries in the region and elsewhere have maintained the share of medium-technology industries in their manufacturing output. Similarly, the contribution of physical-capital intensive products to total exports also declined during this period.[40]

There are flow-ons from this pattern of "while the production of low-technology industries expanded, mainly at the expense of medium-technology industries" for the nature of employment.

The medium and large-scale manufacturing establishments employed some 4 million workers or just 4% of the total work force of around [urban] 90 million. Starting in 1992, manufacturing wages began to rise by about 10% p.a. ... The annual surveys of medium and large-scale manufacturing industries show that the value added-employment elasticity declined from 0.5 in 1989–93 to 0.3 in 1994–97 in the manufacturing sector as a whole, and from 0.4–0.3 to 0.1 in textiles and garments (Table 5.24). The low elasticity in these two relatively labour-intensive industries were the result of very small additions to the workforce, of the order of 1% versus 10%–15% p.a. in the previous period, while continuing to post healthy 10%–15% annual growth rates in output.[41]

Moreover, enterprises of 500 workers or more, employing a third of the workforce, produced 80 per cent of manufacturing value-added. A massive two-thirds of the workforce — 60 million plus — employed in medium (20–99 workers), small scale (5–19 workers) and household industries (1–4 workers) accounted for only 5–6 per cent of total manufacturing value-added.

There is a very large body of research data which confirms the shallow industrialization and the resultant dominance with Indonesian capitalism of small, local enterprises. According to a 2010 research report for USAID: "MSMEs account for over 99 per cent of all firms in all economic sectors and employ over 95 per cent of the population."[42] Consistent with the UNIDO data, USAID confirmed that in 2009, an Asia Foundation survey showed that the mean number of employees per company was 27.6. Although the mean number is relatively high, 70 per cent employed fewer than twenty people while less than 5 per cent employed over 400 workers. Twenty-three companies employed over 1,000 employees with one company, employing 9,000 workers.

There is, however, little easily available mass data documenting the market reach of these enterprises. There is an increasing interest in the process of agglomeration of business in and around the Greater Jakarta area, the north coast of Java between Jakarta and Surabaya, around Surabaya as well as Makassar and Medan.

However, it is clear from the UNIDO and USAID data that this huge proportion of 70 per cent with fewer than twenty people, all using lower levels of technology, *will only be able to service local markets*, especially if they are not linked into one of the agglomerations. Medium to large-scale business becomes metropolitan business and the *rest remain as very local regional business*. Only the conglomerates — the 150 biggest business groups — can claim to be "national", but even there, as indicated earlier, their "national" interests are very unevenly spread and have developed very opportunistically.

This is a fundamental feature of the structure of the Indonesian capitalist class which frames much of the current political life, especially decentralization. There is an opportunistically evolved, mainly ex-crony, small section of the capitalist class, with minimal real national scale and no serious industrial base. Its political power up until 1998 was a result of its status as primarily a crony layer, i.e., protected by the ruling, military-backed, clique-wielding state power. The loss of its political protection has allowed a shift in the balance of power, influence and political initiative within the class and state to the other section of the capitalist class: those located at the local, district or provincial level. This is what has underpinned the emergence of decentralization. The process has been accentuated by other related developments, which I will discuss below in this chapter.

It is the extremely shallow "industrialization" in the Indonesian economy — making Indonesia essentially an unindustrialized economy[43] — that means that Indonesia has no *national* capitalist class operating with a scale, scope and perspective appropriate for a country of Indonesia's geographical, population and political scale. Only strong, rapid industrialization and the level of capital accumulation that it enables could have created such a capitalist class. It is important not to confuse growth in the contribution of manufacturing to GDP with real industrialization.

This is a direct product of Indonesia's semi-colonial underdevelopment, a direct product of colonialism, and is a condition that must be properly understood to grasp any aspect of the country's politics.

While European economic development in the nineteenth and twentieth century was propelled by the industrial revolution and the scientific and technological progress of industry (both in production as well as distribution), the European (and American) imperial powers made sure that their colonies did not share in that revolution. In Indonesia's case, the Netherlands used its colony as a source of mainly agricultural products and mineral outputs. Netherlands capitalists built no serious factories in the East Indies. Even sugar and tobacco mills remained relatively primitive into the twentieth century. When the Indonesian government in 1950 — after the Dutch had ceded sovereignty and the Dutch army and civil service corps left Indonesia — could finally turn more seriously to economic issues, it did so with zero industry. Dutch capital was allowed back, but it was concentrated in plantations, mines, shipping and trade. This is the base from which Indonesia has had to build since 1950. Having no industry means having extremely low labour productivity and no capacity to create and accumulate capital on a scale commensurate with the needs of the country's population, its undeveloped infrastructure and geographic size and realities.

During the period 1950–65, this remained the basic situation. There was a major polarization in the country on how to overcome this backwardness. Sukarno, supported by the Indonesian Communist Party and a big section of the Indonesian National Party, looked to a socialist model, inspired partly by the Chinese economic experiment. This aspiration also required economic cooperation with the Soviet Union and political alliances with states operating with similar policy paradigms. By the 1960s Sukarno was advocating an axis between Jakarta, Phnom Penh, Hanoi, Beijing and Pyongyang. Mohammed Hatta, Indonesia's first vice-president, and Sutan Sjahrir, a prime minister before 1950, had earlier supported a rapid integration of the country into the Western international economic processes, spearheaded by a return and revival of Dutch capital, which was allowed to take back their property and businesses, i.e., their colonial booty. One of the manifestations of the conflict between these two camps was the campaign by the Left to nationalize all Dutch enterprises. This was achieved in 1956–57 as the balance of public support shifted in Sukarno's favour.

The coming to power of the Suharto government in 1965 represented a victory for the path that had been advocated by Hatta and Sjahrir. However while some Dutch capital was invited back (Unilever and Phillips), Suharto's strategy was to rely more on the United States, Japanese and other western European capital. Between 1967 and today, companies from these countries have increased their investment in Indonesia steadily over this period and dominate many sectors. When this process began in 1967–68, the Indonesian capitalist class was tiny, as one might expect in an ex-colony that had been prevented from industrializing. A process began whereby officials (often military) and their associates began accumulating funds through a range of corrupt practices (primitive accumulation), including leveraging their influence to gain equity in new corporations. This practice helped create, by the 1980s, a number of large family business conglomerates who dominated the economic skyline. They were either owned by former officials or by their business associates.[44]

Almost all of these large conglomerates were able to grow because of the close relationships that developed with those wielding power, with Suharto and his family. By the 1990s, the Suharto family business' ability to intervene anywhere in Indonesia's business life was notorious.[45] Habibie's family also developed extended business operations.[46] Several Indonesian Chinese capitalists historically close to Suharto also developed huge businesses. By the 1990s, other figures were also on the scene such as Aburizal Bakrie, Surya Paloh, Hashim Djojohadikusomo, Jusuf Kalla and Hary Tanoesoedibjo. Bakrie is listed no. 6 in the list of the *Globe*'s 150 richest; Hary Tanoesoedibjo no. 17, Hashim no. 37, Jusuf Kalla no. 70, and Paloh no. 91.[47] Another rising star was Dahlan Iskan listed as no. 93. I emphasize these large capitalists in particular because they are the key big businessmen, mostly ex-cronies, who have been striving to play a prominent political role today, usually in a very direct manner. They are the most political of the 150, although there are others who exert political influence through the media, but show no ambitions to become political figures. The long-term New Order figure of Jakob Oetama, of the Gramedia Kompas group, is listed no. 26. He and his *Kompas* group played a central role in the rise and support of Suharto's rule.

During the period both under the New Order and since, including during the period of *desentralisasi*, foreign direct investment has been significant in the country's economic activity.

For most years, including 2013, for example, foreign investment has constituted around 70 per cent of new investments and domestic investment, the remaining 30 per cent. There is little detailed documentation of the lobbying efforts of individual foreign corporations regarding economic policy in general, and governance policies in particular. However, the role of the international financial institutions, such as the International Monetary Fund (IMF), World Bank and ADB, have been to force increased deregulation of investment. This intensified in the period immediately after the 1997 Asian financial crisis and Indonesia's signing of the first Letter of Intent with the IMF. This has facilitated the ongoing entry of foreign investment in almost all sectors — although there is a list of "negative investment" sectors, where direct investment is prohibited and more complex. The most easily identifiable intervention of foreign capital into policy making is at this macro national level where one major thrust has been deregulation of investment. The other very visible priority has been the reduction or abolition of subsidies on a range of commodities (resulting in price rises) as well as reduction in quotas on some agricultural imports.[48]

In discussions with researchers in Indonesia, there has been some expression of concern that the decentralization of some policy-making rights to the kabupaten and municipalities has made it easier for international investors to bypass national oversight bodies and invest directly at the local level. It is difficult to find statistics that can sieve out foreign investments that have been locally done, with no accountability to a national government agency. Certainly, there are reports of bupati doing deals with international investors granting coal, palm oil and other exploration rights in some regions.[49] However, it does not seem likely that there has been a sufficiently substantial opportunistic use of decentralization by international capital to gain access to the regions, avoiding the national government, to emphasize this aspect as central to the onset of *desentralisasi*. It is essentially an internally driven process — while noting the synergies with the ideological predilections of the "donor" technocracy.

Political Economy and Parties

This division of the capitalist class into a small grouping of mainly New Order era big capitalists and a plethora of small, local capital also frame the contemporary party system. In fact, the underdevelopment of the economy and the consequent stunted development of classes has framed the evolution of the party system since independence in a way that reflected the potential for federalism or a decentralized system, under certain conditions. Indonesia's parties, since the end of the guerilla war with the Dutch colonialists, were divided into two camps. There were parties who drew their leadership layers from the land-owning, small capitalist or bureaucratic castes,[50] such as the (right-wing of the) Indonesian Nasional Party (PNI), the Masyumi and the Nahdlatul Ulama. There were several smaller parties like these. There were the parties whose leaders were drawn from the lower intelligentsia (teachers, clerks, journalists, union officials) or directly from the working class and peasantry. The largest of the latter was the Indonesian Communist Party (PKI). The PNI had a left-wing but it was a minority until around 1964.

The parties that drew their leaderships from the capitalist and land-owning class inevitably had a regional orientation. The capitalist class was even more comprised of small local capitalists in the 1950s than it is today. In the 1950s almost all large business was still in Dutch and other foreign hands. There were no Indonesian capitalists with serious commercial operations of any national scale or scope.[51] The Masyumi party had its strongest base in parts of Sumatra and West Java. The landowner-dominated Nahdlatul Ulama was based mostly in East Java and parts of Central Java. Of course, these geographical concentrations also reflected religious and ethnic differences. The PNI in the 1950s was strongest in Central Java, where there was not such a strong, pious Islamic majority. There the PNI tended also to be dominated by larger landowners with family in the civil service. The existence of parties with specific socio-geographic concentrations was precisely a reflection of the fact that they were led and funded by property-owning elites that were local, and not nationally, based. Still encapsulated within local affairs and reality, these local elites spoke to their local support based within existing regional cultural frameworks and vocabularies. The Masyumi, and its close ally, the Indonesian Socialist Party, dominated by Sumatran intellectuals and businessmen, were the parties to most quickly associate themselves with rebellions originating out of regional discontent. They associated themselves closely with the Permesta and PRRI rebellions of 1956–58. These were not separatist rebellions but aimed to establish a new Republic of Indonesia, one which would have had a more federalistic character.

It was the parties with greater links with the non-capitalist classes — the PKI and the PNI, especially through their peasant organizations — that had the most rapid growth in national coverage. Their ideology and vocabulary drew on nationalist and socialist sources rather local religious and cultural outlooks. They began with socio-geographical focus, on Java where the rural landless was greatest, but began to spread rapidly by the 1960s.[52]

During this early period of independent Indonesia's history, the capitalist and land-owning class tended to organize out of regional bases, even when trying to assert themselves in national politics. They have also relied on ideological vocabularies, usually religious, that are identified with different regions. On the other hand, political organizations with worker and peasant bases and agendas quickly adopt national perspectives and ideologies which have no specific regional identification.[53]

The party–class relationship today is still marked by this political economy and political geography, although it underwent restructuring from 1965. There were at least three waves of restructuring which have ramifications for the political geography of the party arrangements and for decentralization today. The first wave was the physical and cultural destruction of the worker and peasant-based parties; the parties that had the strongest national, as distinct from regional identifications and perspectives. The second wave was the "simplification" of the parties which resulted in the shriveling of the organic links between the parties and society, favouring the party of incumbency, Golkar. This underpinned a sense of centralization of power, against any dynamic to decentralization. The third wave, driven mostly by changes in class structure, saw Golkar develop as the party of crony capitalism and the PDI evolve, through a split, into a party independent of cronyism, though still very undefined. This lack of definition was underpinned by the still unrealized assertiveness of local capital. The developments with Golkar consolidated the formal party or representative link between centralistic power and crony capital. The PDI's (later the PDI-P) lack of definition meant that it could not yet play a role providing national agency.

The first wave began when General Suharto, using the pretext of a failed conspiracy to remove and replace the army leadership organized by the PKI's chairman (without the knowledge of his party), seized power in late 1965. He organized a systematic destruction of all leftist supporters of Sukarno.[54] Beginning on 1 October 1965 and lasting around three years, the systematic political murder of around 1 million people took place in Indonesia. The violence was accompanied by mass arrests, with probably hundreds of thousands going in and out of ad hoc prison houses in between 1965 and 1968. Almost 20,000 were kept in prisons and camps until 1979. Murder, torture and imprisonment, accompanied by a sustained propaganda campaign constituted an intense reign of terror. The targets were members and supporters of the PKI, the left wing of the PNI and the mass organizations aligned with them. Also targeted were other smaller left wing parties, such as the Indonesia Party (Partindo) and the Indonesian Communist Movement (ACOMA). The PKI was the largest and most rapidly growing of these forces. Its membership and support base had grown from tens of thousands in the early 1950s to probably more than 20 million people in 1965. By 1965 there were approximately 35–40 million Indonesians of voting age. Sukarno's writings as well as Marxism-Leninism and other leftist writings and ideas were banned. This was followed by thirty years of systematically turning the Indonesian school system into re-education camps which eliminated any memory of the national, class-based politics of Indonesian leftism.[55]

This first wave of restructuring remains effective today, although one can see the seeds of a challenge to its persistence. It has immense importance in terms of the absence of national agency and the dysfunctionality of decentralization. I will return to this question in the final chapter of this essay.

The second wave, "*simplifikasi*", took place during the 1970s and involved forcing the nine non-left political parties, outside of Golkar, to merge into two parties, the Partai Demokrasi Indonesia (PDI) and the Islamic Partai Persatuan Pembangunan (PPP). This created a three-party system: PDI, PPP and Golkar. It was heavily state-managed, ensuring that Golkar remained pre-eminent and that the PDI and PPP leaderships remained pliant. During most of the 1970s and 1980s, Golkar[56] enforced the centralistic rule of the Suharto clique throughout the bureaucracy and pseudo-representative bodies. It was backed up by various forms of military power.

The third wave beginning in the late 1980s and into the 1990s, was the transformation of Golkar into a more direct representation of crony power. The essence of this was, of course, the role of Suharto and his family in Golkar. Apart from Suharto's own dominating position as "Pembina" (a kind of overall supervising patron), his daughter, Tutut, began to play an active role. Other politically ambitious cronies also slowly moved into Golkar. By the last period of the New Order, the regime could very much be categorized as a crony-based regime and Golkar was the formal representational body of the cronies and the bureaucrats linked to them. Meanwhile, beginning in 1991, a new political dynamic developed inside the PDI, often reflecting a dissonance at the local level, among local small capitalists increasingly hostile to key features of the crony regime. It was on this wave of dissonance that Megawati Sukarnoputri rose to the leadership of the PDI, and then PDI-P.[57]

After Suharto

When Suharto fell, the *immediate* party situation was essentially characterized by Golkar, representing KKN (*korupsi, kolusi, nepotisme*) politics facing the PDI-P, representing a still undefined alternative. The PPP quickly fractured into several Islamic parties, none of whom were to grow during the *reformasi* period. Golkar represented centralistic, crony power. It is worth emphasizing again that crony capitalism and centralism always go together both in peoples' perception of politics and in reality. Cronies can only develop their business empires if they are protected by a central political power. Any already existing crony capitalism will also always be allergic to any genuine federal or decentralizing restructuring of the state as it would mean a weakening of the protective agency of the central power. The Suharto regime's centralism was most underlined in public perceptions because of the crony status of his children's businesses and other crony conglomerates. Within the civil service and technocracy, there was an awareness of the need to localize the implementation of policy. The centralistic character of the regime was more associated with the centralization of privilege and the subordination of the state's repressive apparatus to protecting that centralization of privilege both against rivals, and threats from below.

This is why the PDI-P could emerge as the main opposition party in the parliament but also be against federalism and over-decentralization. The centralization was not perceived as regional, but personal, clique and crony-based.[58] The PDI-P will later develop (as of 2013 onwards) reflecting a new axis of national–local politics. However, in 1998–99, it was a reluctant supporter of any decentralization. The pro-federal sentiment comes from the old Masyumi base, from Amien Rais and his National Mandate Party (PAN), with its strong bases in Sumatra and West Java and from specific formations representing regional elites, like those which emerged in East Kalimantan.

However, the implications for national–local political relations in the evolution of party politics since the fall of Suharto go beyond the early pro and anti-federal tensions between PDI-P, Golkar and PAN. Moreover, it is crucial to understand that this evolution is ongoing, having to deal with the tensions embedded in the restructures that took place during the New Order period. This evolution relates to both the changing relationships within the capitalist class (ex-crony versus local, smaller capitalist) and the issue of the absence of party organization for non-capitalist classes. Both have enormous implications for national agency and thus national–local relationships.

My argument from the start of this essay has been that decentralization is a manifestation of the changed balance of power between (ex)-crony capital and local, smaller capital. The change takes place as cronies become ex-cronies with the loss of their protector. This loss of protector also starts a process which impacts on the political organizing of the (ex)-cronies, which hitherto had been done through Golkar under the patronage of Suharto. In 1999, and to a certain extent in 2004, this was still the case. However, the fundamental trend from 1999 until 2013 has been for the break-up of the cronies as a single political bloc.

When Suharto was forced to resign in May 1998, these conglomerates were deprived of their patron. The 1999 elections also quickly revealed that Golkar was no longer able to dominate the political terrain. The conglomerates remained significant commercial players and sources of financial resources, despite several of them being devastated in the 1997 financial crisis. However, from 1998 onwards their status as "crony conglomerates" ceased. Since 1999 they have had to subordinate themselves to a new principle of Indonesian politics: the electoral principle. Positions in the government became dependent on electoral results. Elections were held without a condition of repression, which meant that direct vote buying steadily decreased in importance. This new condition that the conglomerates faced was deepened with the introduction of direct elections for the president and vice-president as well as for heads of local government.

Crony capitalism is dependent on the existence of a single authoritarian ruler or clique who chooses and maintains or allows crony capitalists to exist and grow by protecting their access to business opportunities, in particular deals that can be accessed via the state. The end of the dictatorship ended that situation. Competition among capitalists for access to state resources under crony capitalism takes the form of competition for access to the figure at the top of the pyramid. Much of the political history of the Indonesian elite is a history of the rise and fall from favoured status in the eyes of Suharto for various figures. This was also reflected in the rise and fall of access to business opportunities. However, by 1998 key business cronies, most starkly represented by Aburizal Bakrie, also began manoeuvring for direct political position. This was no doubt brought about by the awareness that, at some point, Suharto must retire or die. After 1996 as a political crisis developed, the possibility of Suharto going due to other reasons also would have become a factor. Other conglomerate figures, such as Surya Paloh and Hashim Djojohadikusumo, also entered the political fray more directly. Paloh built a major media empire that intervened significantly into politics via the news reporting on its television station. Hashim's brother, Prabowo Subianto, was a strategically placed military officer who began to take his own initiatives in the political arena. In the 1990s — almost until May 1998 — the framework for all of these figures' political activity was competing to win favour from and to defend Suharto. They competed for access to favour but they were also a relatively united bloc in defence of the Suharto era status quo.

The electoral politics of the post-Suharto scenario ended that situation. The conglomerates remained in commercial competition with each other but they ceased to operate as a united political bloc. Within less than a decade all of the key crony figures who had moved into politics have established their own political parties. In the immediate post Suharto period key conglomerate figures were all still based in Golkar. This has been a talking point in the social media in 2013 with the circulation of a photo of Prabowo, Bakrie and Surya Paloh clasping hands with Akbar Tandjung and Wiranto at a Golkar event and all in their yellow Golkar jackets. Jusuf Kalla was also a key Golkar figure at that time. In this early period there were a series of struggles for control of Golkar or at least to be the primary Golkar figure. Bakrie emerged as the winner and, as of April 2014, is the Golkar presidential hopeful. Jusuf Kalla remains a rival in the wings having his own network inside and outside Golkar. Prabowo and Paloh left Golkar and have established their own parties, Gerindra and Nasional Demokrat respectively. Another conglomerate capitalist, Hary Tanoesoedibjo, was originally cooperating with Paloh in Nasional Demokrat, but has more recently shifted to Hanura, the party of General Wiranto. The originally Surabaya-based New Order conglomerate figure, Dahlan Iskan, has served in the cabinet of Yudhoyono and so is a Partai Demokrat figure. The emergence of the Partai Demokrat, as a vehicle for Yudhoyono, in 2004, and its eight-year incumbency, attracting some conglomerate figures such as Iskan, adds another cleavage among big conglomerate capital. There is absolutely no longer any political solidarity among this crony sector of big capital. Their political role as the solid defender of the crony regime status quo under Suharto has disappeared and their underlying rivalry appears.

Of course, the ending of political power for the core clique of cronies, the Suharto family itself, is also central to the crumbling of this political bloc. Suharto's children remain wealthy, and Tommy Suharto is still listed no. 69 and Suharto's daughter Siti Hardiyanti Rukmana (Tutut) no. 135 in the *Globe Asia's* richest 150. However, their political clout has disappeared. They have both tried to gain leadership inside Golkar at different times, but failed. They have both tried sponsoring small, new parties but have achieved no significant political profile. Their departure from or reduced role in Golkar and sponsorship of their own parties are another manifestation in the unravelling of the conglomerate bloc, once they cease being actual cronies.

The break-up of the cronies as a political bloc, organized in Suharto's Golkar during the New Order, has seen the collapse of Golkar from a party that scored always between 65 and 70 per cent of the vote to one with a national vote under 20 per cent. As Golkar has shrunk, so too has its geographic base. No longer the party of the ruling crony regime, it too devolves backwards to a party with essentially regional bases. In fact, in the face of the absence of a serious-sized, *national* capitalist class, all of Indonesia's political parties remain, essentially regionally based, as the map in Figure 1 illustrates. There is, of course, no national working class or peasant party yet established that could challenge this regionalization.

There is yet another crucial feature of how party politics has developed which reflects the shift in the balance of power between ex-crony, conglomerate capital and local, smaller capital. This is the way in which the local political situation, i.e., the position of local elite figures, determines alliances between parties at the local level, irrespective of the national relations between parties or between their ideologies. Throughout Indonesia, almost every possible combination of political parties has been formed during and after election campaigns. These often do not reflect the coalition that operates in the national parliament and is the basis of the Yudhoyono government.

Not only do coalitions between parties not reflect the coalitions that exist on the national level, they also seem to be ideologically compatible despite the differences that might be assumed from their formal ideological rhetoric. Buehler and Tan, looking at the 2004 local elections, found a variety of alliances

FIGURE 1

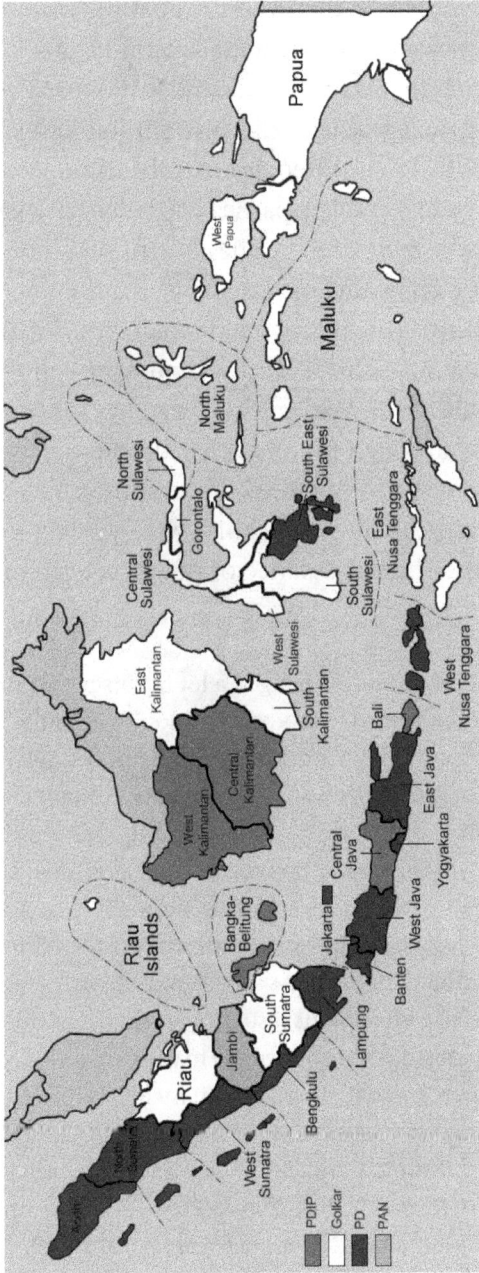

Source: Accessed from <http://en.wikipedia.org/wiki/File:2009_ElectionsIndonesia.png>.

even within a province, like in South Sulawesi, including alliances between the pluralist, non-sectarian, semi-secular PDI-P and the Islamic fundamentalist Prosperous and Justice Party (PKS) in some *kabupaten*.[59] Choi's study of Riau also shows, for example, PDI-P in alliance with PAN, otherwise usually in opposition to each other.[60] Relations between parties at the local level often boil down to relations between cliques organized around individual businessmen or bureaucratic families.

More recently Buehler documented some of the processes in the emergence of local family cliques in Banten, West Java and South Sulawesi.[61] Within the different clans, there was less party fluidity, although his research indicates that feuds between families *at the local level* find their expressions in opposing national party affiliations. More significantly were Buehler's observations confirming the shift in balance of power between national and local power structures. He writes:

Things might not have changed a lot in this regard since 2005, but this still means that the composition of local powerholders is now quite different from what it was under Suharto's New Order regime. Leaving aside one obvious similarity — the fact that women constitute a small minority among candidates competing in these races both before and after 1998 — the pool of candidates and winners during both the first and second rounds of *pilkada* looks rather different compared to the New Order. During Suharto's 32-year reign, military personnel and *national* level civil servants, usually parachuted in from another province or district, constituted the majority of local government heads. Now, candidates with a military and police background are almost entirely absent in these races as are candidates from "outside" a district. Candidates these days were usually born in the locality in which they compete for power. In other words, these are races, by and large, between "local boys".

With large conglomerate capital and the old repressive apparatus that protected it unravelled, and — most importantly — its vehicle as a political bloc, Golkar, no longer such a vehicle, local families combining bureaucratic position and business have the initiative. The break-up of the ex-crony political bloc into rival parties has additional ramifications given the shift in Indonesia to an election-based system. Even these conglomerate-funded parties become dependent on local business: they need figures, with local profile and networks, for candidates. The centralized protective power operating under Suharto's crony regime separated big crony capital from any "organic" relations with other layers of society. Their access to society at large was through the bureaucracy. In post-Suharto Indonesia, this does remain a factor and is reflected in the desire to make bureaucratic incumbency as secure as possible. This is also documented in Buehler's "Married with Children" article where he documents local elite families strategizing to dominate different levels of representative and administrative power so as to secure long-term incumbency. He writes:

> holding strategic positions at *different* levels of government as well as in both executive *and* legislative branches of government seems to improve the chances of family electoral success. This is aptly shown in the case of Banten province. There, Ratu Atut's husband, Hikmat Tomet became the head of the provincial Golkar party branch after he won a seat for the party in the legislative elections in 2009. He has used this position to ensure that all the family's candidates were placed first in the Golkar list of candidates in the constituencies where they are running in the 2014 legislative elections.

In the cases that Buehler documents, a party like Golkar "consolidates" its position in Banten and South Sulawesi but through a *desentralisasi* of its own structures. It becomes geographically tied to that region almost by coincidence, depending on whatever links with local dynasties — bureaucrats and capitalists — can be established.

Anational Political Format

In some ways, the political economy and party map that I have sketched above portrays an *anational* political format. A domestic capitalist class comprising a rivalry-ridden small layer of ex-cronies and other big capital and a mass of small and middle-sized, locally based capitalists are incapable — so far — of creating any genuinely national political parties. Alliances established at the national level are often undermined at the local level. The "national" parties' geographical spread depends almost on accidental linkages in this or that region. In day-to-day politics, political vocabularies are adopted adapting to the cultural backgrounds dominant in different regions, something which is directly reflected in the formal profiles of religious parties.

The absence of political parties, or social movements, coming directly out of the non-capitalist classes deepens further this *anational* character. Not yet existing, they obviously provide no alternative, thus also not acting as a reason for unity, ideologically or otherwise, among the popular classes. In this *anational* political format, decentralization finds fertile soil. This *anational* situation also helps to exacerbate the dysfunctional aspects of decentralization. Without a national capitalist class of serious scope and weight, it is the policies of the international financial institutions that set the macro-economic framework.

Chapter III

Decentralization:
Its Discontents

In assessing the impact of *desentralisasi*, it can be viewed in at least two ways — as a manifestation of a change in the political balance flowing from changes in the political economy or as the implementation of a (technocratic) policy to improve economic and social development. The analysis in the previous two chapters presents the emergence of decentralization as primarily a manifestation of changes in the political side of the political economy. In an under-industrialized economy comprising a plethora of small- and medium-sized local capitalists and a tiny conglomerate sector (for the size of the country), the end of the crony regime and the consequent privileged position of crony capital has unleashed a dynamic giving more room to move for the smaller, local capitalists. This is the essence of *desentralisasi*. It is the basis for a more *anational* political format.

Perhaps *anational* is a difficult concept to use. The Indonesian nation, as a stable community inhabiting clear borders (though disputed in western Papua), with a common language, economic and cultural life, certainly continues to exist, even if with lowered expectations for itself than previously held. There is a national government which, despite *desentralisasi*, controls the majority of the nation's state revenues and sets the policy frameworks, in which local governments must operate. It is perhaps also further complicated by the dominance of classical liberal and neo-liberal economic policy thought in Indonesia, which emphasizes market mechanisms rather than intervention by the national state. This may not be so much a complicating factor, but rather a reinforcing factor. In the absence of a strong national social class providing direction for the nation, an ideology emphasizing a smaller role for the state finds a comforting environment *at elite levels.* The New Order government may have pursued an agenda which included prioritizing protecting the privileges of crony capitalists but the powerful character of the core military rule established in the 1960s and 1970s also meant that it could impose a national direction. At least until the early 1980s, the so-called Berkeley Mafia technocrats through BAPPENAS (National Development Planning Authority) imposed a national economic direction. There was a national ideology: *Pembangunan* (Development), at least until the Asian financial crisis of 1997 and the Indonesian *krismon* (monetary crisis) exposed that "development" was impossible (under current strategy).

During the period of *reformasi* and *desentralisasi*, there has been no sense of national economic direction or national economic ideology. Almost nobody mentions BAPPENAS anymore. This is not because the Yudhoyono government has not formulated economic "master plans". Under Hatta Rajasa, Coordinating Minister for Economic Affairs, the government has both a Master Plan for the Acceleration and Expansion of Indonesian Economic Development and a National Long-Term Development Plan (RPJPN – 2002–2025).[62] However these "national" economic "plans" and initiatives have won almost no major profile or generated any political interest or discourse. The only national economic decisions that have generated national political debate have been the decisions to increase the price of fuel. Other national "debates" have emerged only in relation to matters that have occurred in response to international market developments, such as the drop in the value of the rupiah accounting for the rise in the price of soya beans. The fundamental parameters that confine economic policy formulation are those that were acquiesced to during the New Order formulated by the "donor" powers, first through the Inter-governmental Group on Indonesia (later renamed the Consultative group on Indonesia) and, after 1997, through the numerous Letters of Intent signed by Indonesian governments as part of an agreement to IMF requirements. This acquiesence over the last forty years has steadily deregulated the environment for large foreign capital while at the same time also reducing the state's previous activities in holding down prices. Infringements on this free marketism do occur; however, in a very mild form. Domestic business interests can stir up nationalistic demands for limitations on foreign capital but they are usually minor, short-lived and then often further moderated at the last moment when final policy is determined. Free-market spirited *ideology* is hegemonic, even as individual conglomerate owners fantasize about becoming a crony again, such as by becoming president.

While left, progressive-oriented NGOs and researchers raise nationalist critiques from time to time, the public discussion around economic activity that dominates in the media is more often connected to the social safety net populism and other initiatives of mayors and *bupati*, with that of Joko Widodo being the most prominent. However, other mayors and *bupati*, such as in Jembrana, or Lampung or Surabaya also attract similar attention. The irony here is that most of these local officials have won profiles for their social safety net policies, such as increased budget for free health and education services for the poorest layers of the populations in their cities.[63] In all these cases, the policies themselves as well as the budget for the policies were the result of decisions made at the national level. Very few local governments have been able to raise substantial funds at the local level and are dependent on the transfers of funds from the national government. There is little doubt the period of *desentralisasi* has been accompanied by political atmospherics where there is a palpable lack of national projects or directions. It has become a commonplace in conversations to talk of a government on "auto-pilot" or of a presidency which is characterized essentially only by expressions of *"keprihatinan"* (sympathy and concern) as major problems emerge.

It is not that a policy of devolving budgetary and some policy authority to local government in and of itself militates against the national government taking national major initiatives or winning a profile for initiatives it may have been taken. The issue is what underpins the hegemony of *desentralisasi* politics, namely the absence of any strong social class with a national perspective. The problem is not necessarily devolution of some authority to local government but *the devolution of such power in a class structure situation which is not producing any social force capable of acting as a national agency in pursuing economic, social or political strategies*, for whatever class.

One response to this argument is that the *desentralisasi* itself is a national initiative which suits Indonesia's development needs and will promote progress in the economy. Pepinsky and Wihardja[64] have undertaken some useful research to answer this assertion, which I will discuss below. However, it is worth emphasizing the extent to which arguments that *desentralisasi* will be an effective pro-development approach, place all their hope in "the market" and give little weight to the social and economic problems related to the social, economic and administrative unevenness in this huge island archipelago. Indonesia contains resource rich and resource poor islands and parts of islands. It contains islands and parts of islands with different levels of economic development and rural-urban balances. There are different levels in the development of human resource development depending on what educational institutional resources are available. The rationale behind the idea that *desentralisasi* itself will be a solution to Indonesia's poverty and economic backwardness completely negates any idea that *co-ordination* may be needed to level the human, natural and institutional resource unevenness across the archipelago.

Pepinsky and Wihardja succinctly sum up the arguments justifying *desentralisasi*.

> The first claim is that inter-jurisdictional competition forces all local governments to adopt better policies. The second claim is that local democracy forces local governments to adopt better policies.[65]

Pepinsky and Wihardja argue that their research shows that "neither of these two mechanisms has worked consistently across local governments". The first of these claims is the market-based justification that governments will *compete* and that it will be this competition that will drive more productive outputs, assuming that local governments will act as companies are expected to do. The second claim is based on an assumption that the introduction of direct elections will actually improve the quality of democracy. Their work does not take into account the absence of any process of reorganization of non-capitalist classes and that absence's impact on democratic processes. However, as I will note later, they do raise the issue of the impact of a weak "civil society", though in a very abstract manner.

Overall, they conclude that there has been no impact on macroeconomic performance reflected in GDP figures. In Figure 2, they show that real GDP growth under Suharto's centralized New Order system and under decentralization has not been different. They see *desentralisasi* as having brought no significant change at all to the country's economic performance.

FIGURE 2

Indonesia, Yearly Per Capita Real GDP Growth, 1991–2007

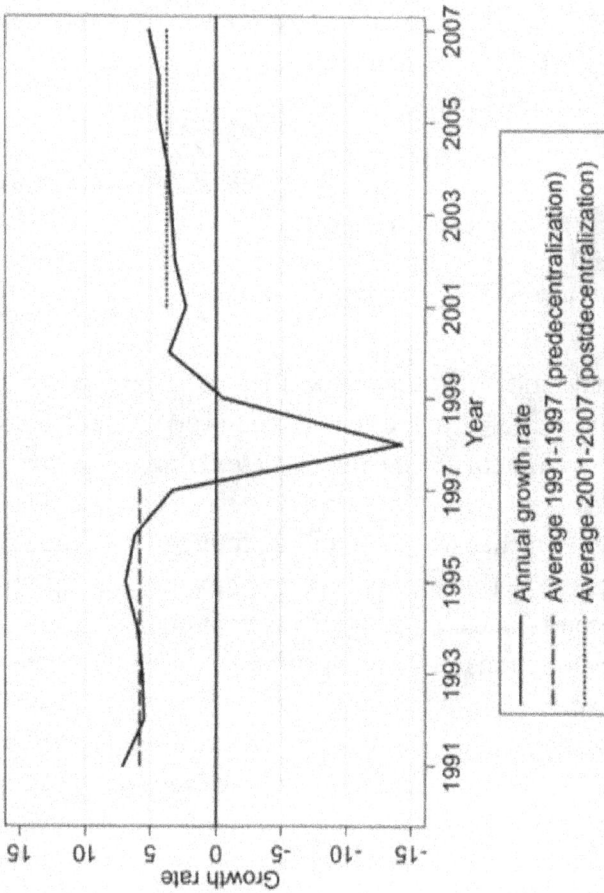

Source: Thomas Pepinsky and Maria Wihardja, "Decentralization and Economic Performance in Indonesia", *Journal of East Asian Studies* 11 (2011): 337–71.

Pepinsky and Wihardja do not raise the issue on the unevenness of social, economic and institutional development as a development planning or co-ordination problem. However, they de facto register this unevenness — which they refer to as "heterogeneity" in "proximity to trade routes", "geography and human capital" — as a key reason why the expected competition between regions has not produced improved economic performance. They present their commentary on this issue of heterogeneity to explain a framework as follows:

> Under decentralization, local governments are free to experiment and innovate; those governments that respond to market demands to provide good policies will attract capital, and those that fail to adopt good policies will not. Seeing this, the latter group of governments will adopt policies that resemble the former.[66]

They continue, noting that such results will:

> Depend critically on the assumption that jurisdictional units are sufficiently similar for competition to be feasible.[67]

They ask:

> Are Indonesia's regions similar enough to one another that all regions can feasibly compete for the same productive resources? We argue that they are not.[68]

In their study, they use examples relating to geography as well as uneven development of human resources. They point to the advantages that Batam Town, on Batam island, right next to Singapore, has, compared to almost anywhere else in the archipelago. The policies that the Batam local government introduced (with national government support, it should be noted) could not be copied anywhere else in Indonesia. Batam is a typical example of a resource-rich region — in so far as proximity to Singapore should be seen as a resource factor. The authors are right, of course, that policies implemented to maximize exploitation of different, specific natural resources cannot be adopted by other regions which do not have such resources. The dynamic of regions being able to "adopt policies that resemble" booming regions is fictitious.

The other example they use relates to the uneven development of human resources, referring to literacy rates.

> Human capital endowments differ starkly as well, both across regions and within them. Across provinces, adult literacy rates in 2005 ranged from a high of 98.87 per cent in North Sulawesi to a low of 71.48 per cent in Papua. Within the province of Central Java, local literacy rates range from a high of 96.53 per cent in Kota Salatiga to a low of 74.89 per cent in the *kabupaten* of Sragen. While it is certainly possible that governments in Salatiga and Sragen could each adopt investment friendly policies, it is unlikely that any sort of policy innovation in Sragen could entice forms in need of a skilled workforce to relocate from Salatiga.[69]

Pepinsky and Wihardja highlight a second cause for decentralization's failure to improve economic performance. This is "factor mobility". Both of them see this problem as separate but additional to "heterogeneity". They see it as a factor that inhibits the effectiveness of any competition between local governments which becomes possible as a result of decentralization. Looking at "factor mobility", they conclude that:

> These results call into question whether labour mobility is sufficient to force local governments to compete with one

another to offer good policies. We estimate that fewer than 40 per cent of Indonesians would actually move in search of better work. And although standard economic considerations do shape Indonesians' willingness to move, we find no evidence that what inter-jurisdictional labour mobility does exist conforms to the logic of competing for labour by offering good policies.[70]

They also point out that mineral and agricultural resources are "quite simply immobile" and this again, they argue, means that the model of competition between local governments to make good policy becomes ineffective.

They sum-up by concluding:

> The lower bound of our estimates is the productive assets underlying more than 30 per cent of Indonesia's private sector GDP are immobile. We see no evidence that this trend has declined over the short period of time under consideration. While the majority of Indonesia's GDP is still potentially mobile under this definition, the fact that such a substantial portion of Indonesia's economic output consists of assets that are immobile calls into question the ability of decentralization (or any other political innovation to have forced local governments to compete over them).[71]

They note rather that this immobility of some resources has tempted some local governments into finding ways that they can be taxed for no other reason that they cannot move away.

Hetereogenity, Mobility and Coordination

Pepinsky and Wihardja's analysis is a sober but very conventional assessment of decentralization's impact on economic performance, in particular, raising national or local GDP. It assessed the new policies within the frameworks mostly argued

for from within the technocracy and donor institutions. All of
the literature they draw on comes from these sources. Their
arguments make sense but perhaps the phenomenon they refer to
might also be analysed in a different framework. Their examples
of heterogeneity and even of mobility both emphasize what
I referred to earlier in this section as the unevenness in both
the natural and human resources of the archipelago. Certain
unevenness exists in all countries, but in a country such as
Indonesia this uneven development is extreme. This is partly a
function of the country's size and the diversity in habitat and
natural resources spread across an archipelago wider than the
United States. This geographical spread combined with location
has also placed different parts of Indonesia on different trade
routes. There is an astounding diversity. Furthermore, economic
underdevelopment, originating out of the colonial economy, has
left very big disparities in level of manufacture and institutional
development, some of which Pepinsky and Wihardja referred
to. Their analysis however has no alternative way to treat
this unevenness and diversity. They end their study with the
following conclusion:

> For decentralization to foster national development, a country
> must have relatively homogenous regions, highly mobile
> labor and capital, and strong accountability for local leaders.
> Indonesia's experience demonstrates how the absence of
> these three requirements can hamstring decentralisation's
> effectiveness, particularly in the very districts where good
> governance is most needed.[72]

While they are firm, and convincing, on their assessment of the
impact of decentralization, their approach neither yields nor even
points to any other possible solutions. They indeed emphasize:
"In closing, we hasten to add that none of our findings imply

that the opposite of decentralization — centralization — is a superior route to increased national performance". They explain that they found neither negative nor positive impacts from decentralization.

The two features of Indonesia which they consider were obstacles to decentralization having a positive impact — and there is a third which I will discuss below separately — are absolutely fundamental features of Indonesian reality. If heterogeneity and unevenness are obstacles to decentralization fostering national development, and recentralization is ruled out for democratic as well as commonsensical reasons to ways of dealing with this unevenness, is there an alternative approach? Also at the level of common sense, a country which exhibits extreme unevenness in levels of natural and human resource development, as well as being geographically fragmented, it would seem that the key idea to be grasped is that in these circumstances there needs to be maximum coordination: i.e., *the maximum capacity to even out the unevenness through mutually beneficial inter-actions, including transfers of resources of all kinds, according to the different needs of different areas.* Such an approach, of course, would require both high levels of planning at the national level as well as high levels of local input to decision making in being able to help determine accurately what local needs are and how local resources can be injected into a national mix.

Given that there are 508 *kabupaten* and municipalities in Indonesia,[73] it is almost impossible at this stage to have systematic data depicting the extent of mutual as well as destructive interaction between these *kabupaten* under the new system over the last decade of decentralization. However, there are already numerous anecdotal reports of destructive rivalries between districts, as well as between district and the provincial as well as national levels of government. The kinds of incidents that are reported include the issuing of business regulations that constrain businesses from inter-*kabupaten* activity, such as in the transport and freight sector; better public facilities (such as hospitals) being accessed by better off residents of neighbouring districts; as well as differing regulations impacting on local revenue gathering. There are also reports of successful collaborations between other segments of local governments on some issues.[74] These kinds of ad hoc unevenness as well as connectivity again pose the challenge of greater coordination and planning as part of fostering national development.

Pursuing an argument along these lines would bring us in to a discussion of different approaches to national development, and the arguments for and against planning as against markets. That is a huge debate and is not the focus of this essay. However, what I think can be emphasized even for an initial reflection on the problem of addressing the "heterogeneity" combined with "factor immobility" is that if there is also a lack of a social force with a serious national presence and perspective, the challenge of overcoming this unevenness in a way that can foster national development appears even more enormous. Here again we return to the class structure and forces that frame Indonesian politics and policy formulation. Labour is only just beginning to awaken. The social composition of the capitalist class is characterized by the present specific balance between a small (compared to the scale of the society) and politically divided ex-crony layer of big capitalists alongside an ocean of smaller, locally based capitalists with the political initiative in their hands because of the end of crony privilege. There is no effective social class force with a national perspective. In this situation, while *national political agency based on an effective social force* remains absent, the prospects of achieving coordination and the optimal mutually beneficial usage of resources will continue to be hamstrung. The question on the emergence of such agency — the reality we are examining is itself defined by process not by a static reality — will be discussed further in the concluding chapter of this essay.

Pepinsky and Wihardja themselves do vaguely and indirectly touch on the question of weak agency when they discuss the third obstacle to decentralization impacting positively on economic performance: "endogenous institutional quality". Under this heading, they discuss issues such as levels of education and competence of local officials, the general strength of a range of social and political institutions operating at the local level, as well as corruption and what they refer to as "local capture", i.e., the capture of local government by business interests, an issue which we have also discussed earlier using material from Buehler describing the situation in Banten and West Java. Some of the material that Pepinsky and Wihardja present on the relationship between local competence levels and project outcomes seems commonsensical. Thus, for example, they describe how a seed planting project works in one district but not in another because the seeds were planted in the wrong season by improperly trained officials. However, the data they presented was minimal and anecdotal in the extreme. More significant, and strengthened by the pictures developed by both Buehler and Hadiz, for example, are data relating to corruption. Pepinsky and Wihardja stated the following regarding corruption at the local level:

> Because local leaders are now directly elected (as opposed to appointed) local business elites can also fund political campaign in return for preferential regulations once these candidates are elected. The result is local capture of economic and/or political institutions by local business and political elites. ... As of February 2011, 30 per cent of Indonesia's 524 local administrators are under investigation as "graft suspects" (*Jakarta Post*, 1 March 2011). It is undeniable that local direct elections have been

marred by money politics and political corruption due to the opportunities for business elites to fund local campaigns.[75]

Buehler confirms the pressure for this extraordinary level of admitted corruption:

> Even before they start campaigning, candidates normally have to pay parties several hundred thousand dollars just to get nominated.[76]

In addition to this, distributing cash handouts to potential voters is still common. All this money has to be recouped.

Buehler also gave examples of "local capture" in his descriptions of Banten, West Java and South Sulawesi. One of the most striking, and a typical example of the many stories circulating is the case he gave for Banten district on Java:

> Both the Atut and Limpo family have roots in their respective provinces that reach deep into the New Order period. Ratu Atut's father, Chasan Sochib was born in Serang district in 1930. In 1967, he started to provide logistical support to the Siliwangi military division. In 1969, he founded the PT Sinar Ciomas Raya construction company, which today is one of the biggest contractors in the province, carrying out construction projects financed by the government as well as donor agencies, such as the Asia Development Bank and the World Bank. Sochib also laid his hands on real estate, moved into tourism and profited from the privatization of Krakatau Steel, one of the few industrial sites in the province. The family's "silverback" also became the director of the Banten branch of the Indonesian National Contractors Association (Gapensi), the head of the province's Construction Business Development Committee (Lembaga Pengembangan Jasa Konstruksi) as well as head of

the Regional Chamber of Commerce (Kadin). Despite Sochib's death in 2011, the family holds a quasi-monopoly over these organizations until today.[77]

Such a case is also reminiscent of the earlier material presented by Hadiz in *Localising Power* for North Sumatra and East Java. Certainly, corruption has reached extraordinary levels throughout local governments. As the 2011 figures quoted by Pepinsky and Wihardja indicate, the figures on this are staggering. In August, 2012 *Tempo* magazine quoted the Ministry of Home Affairs reporting 277 governors, mayors and *bupati* as being involved in corruption.[78] The Ministry also registered 431 of the 2008 members of provincial parliaments as being involved in corruption cases. 2,553 district heads, from a total of 16,267, were also registered as being caught up in corruption.

Later in December 2012, the Directorate for Regional Autonomy in the Ministry issued another list:[79]

Governors	20
Deputy Governors	7
Bupati	156
Deputy *Bupati*	46
Mayors	41
Deputy Mayors	20
Total officials	290
Kabupaten and Municipal parliaments	431
Provincial parliaments	2,545
Total parliament members	2,976
Regional government officials	1,221

Pepinsky and Wihardja, as well as Buehler and Hadiz, underline the connection between the introduction of local elections and the funding of campaigns by local business as a key entry point for the spread of this corruption. There are at least two other features of the situation which contribute to this in important ways. One of these is connected to the fundamental political economy issues that I have raised in this essay and the other to the non-electoral, more administrative and budgetary aspects of the decentralization policies. First, it has to be noted that in the under-industrialized Indonesian economy, even as the economy has grown in absolute size, capital accumulation in Indonesia remains limited. The primitive accumulation of cash (not necessarily capital), i.e., corruption, and the establishment of nepotistic and collusive relations with the major sources of funds, i.e., government, is unavoidable. It is an inevitable result of the extreme under-capitalization from the plethora of Indonesian small and medium enterprises.[80]

Secondly, it is not simply the procedure of direct elections that has opened up greater prospects for corruption but the devolution of funds to the districts. Furthermore, the package of decentralization policies has also created a labyrinth of decision-making processes allowing many entry-points for interventions from sources external to the local formal processes. There are two fronts where this has opened up. Firstly, there is the quagmire as a result of decentralization still being semi-federal. Funds and decision-making authority have been devolved to the *kabupaten* and municipal level, to the *kabupaten* and municipal parliament and mayor and *bupati's* offices. Implementation of programmes is still, however, carried out within the framework of national ministries. It is the district offices (*dinas*) of national ministries that will have to carry out the decisions of *kabupaten* level government and parliament. These may come into conflict with the priorities pursued by the Ministry's national office, or even the parliamentary committee overseeing that Ministry's budget.

At the local level itself, the *bupati* as well as the parliament, and its various committees, have influence over what projects and programmes will receive budgets. The points at which projects and priorities can be pushed therefore include the national ministerial office, the national parliamentary committee overseeing the ministry, *bupati, kabupaten* parliamentary committees, as well as *dinas* officials. Given that parliamentary committees can comprise members from up to five or six parties, all of whom have received funding from businesses; it is not surprising that there are many reports of huge discrepancies between plans formulated by district development planning officials and what is actually implemented. Foreign businesses can also intervene through these interstices. The specifics of the labyrinths are different from region to region. Given that some aspects of decentralization have only been in practice for less than ten years, much of the picture of what happens on the grounds in this labyrinth relies on data from early research and anecdotes.[81]

The technocratic analysis and solutions to this can give a different bent. Hofman, Kaiser and Schulze, analysts with World Bank backgrounds, concluded in their essay on "Corruption and Decentralization" that "overall corruption levels have not altered much on impact of the decentralization".[82] Their analysis is based on responses from surveys and they do not include the record of arrests and court cases. They are cautious, to some extent, in generalizing and point out that the business sector may have different views.[83] As with many of the technocratic approaches, solutions to whatever significant corruption and corruption-related inefficiencies which they did identify are restricted to specific policy reforms that government can carry out. These include, in the assessments of these authors, police reform, publication of budget details, transparent procurement and other procedures, "credible rating systems", and "continuous research on development".[84]

Even these technocratic analysts do mention that one "general finding pertains to the high relative importance of political factors".[85] It is worth quoting in full how they see the relevant examples as a contrast with Pepinsky and Wihardja, and especially Buehler's approaches.

> That evaluation by the business community suggests that the Indonesian investment climate is still far from normal conditions, under which economic endowment variables (regarding the availability and costs of labour, infrastructure, human capital, etc.) would have a greater weight. Manufacturing in particular is prone to illegal levies, either by government officials or the surrounding community (mass organizations, village youth or gangsters). Trade and service industries encounter discrimination when securing their business licences. Small and medium-scale businesses receive poorer services than large-scale operations. There are widespread complaints about retributions, taxes and other local levies that are unfriendly to the business community. Also the uncertainty on regulations, procedures, time, and tariff structure is seen as a major obstacle to the business community.[86]

Again their solutions are policy reforms that government can carry out such as the introduction of "open list elections" ending party candidate lists, which they argue would allow voters to choose competent individuals rather than be forced to accept party machine candidates. Their other suggested political reform is the holding of referenda, although they do not discuss examples of this.

None of these kinds of reforms deal with either the obstacles to fostering national development that Pepinsky and Wihardja identified, let alone the fundamental class power issues underpinning the whole character of decentralization that I have identified. Hofman, Kaiser and Schulze see the problems in terms of policy and institutional weaknesses. There is no discussion or identification of political agency, i.e., whether there is a mobilizable social force that could act as an agency for change, even of the limited kind they describe. Pepinsky and Wihardja do touch on this subject but in a limited and tentative way, and not in relation to any aspects of national coordination of developmental processes. In their material on institutional quality they point to what they claim as positive experiences in:

> Co-operative relationships between public officials and private stakeholders, generating proinvestment and prodevelopment outcomes.[87]

The kind of example they refer to, but have not documented, are "regular socialization events" where local executives inform attending citizens of policy plans and implementation. However, while explaining that the issue was "beyond the scope of this article", they did feel it worth noting a point made in the *2010 Human Development Report* that is related to agency:

> Civil society organizations can also curb the excesses [sic] of markets and the state. In Indonesia non-governmental organizations (NGOs), the press and trade unions pressured the state to expand political freedoms and deliver poverty reduction programmes after the 1997 financial crisis.[88]

This statement is somewhat questionable in terms of historical accuracy and precision. There were no activists or influential trade unions in 1997, and the press was mainly muzzled. It is, however, true that mobilized students and sections of the informal proletariat were able to create a street protest movement sufficiently strong to overthrow the authoritarian regime under Suharto and establish a new political environment where independent trade unions and more freedom of speech have been a factor. Even with this questionable precision of description, however, Pepinsky and Wihardja do dare a generalization on this topic:

> These remarks illustrate some key considerations for decentralized Indonesia.... that a strong civil society — which should be the consequence of democratization, not decentralization — may be the key to making decentralization work.

Strangely, although stated here as the "key" to "making decentralization work", they engage in no further discussion on the implications of their statement. Like almost all the discussion on decentralization, ideas for solutions to problems remain limited to policy reform tinkering, capacity building or, on the other hand, have no solutions. There is an avoidance of precisely those questions identified as, indeed, "key".

Furthermore, even this limited reference to agency, at least in terms of reform pressure, is related narrowly to the problem addressing corruption and other manifestations of low "institutional quality". They do not raise the issue of the role of "civil society" — to use their terminology — in addressing issues of "heterogeneity" or "factor immobility", i.e., the problem of decentralizing in an unevenly resourced and developed, huge archipelagic country.

Chapter IV

National Agency and a "Co-ordinative State": The Future of Decentralization

The case of East Kalimantan, namely a non-ethnically based call by a regional elite for a federal state, points to a major change in how the decentralized structuring of the Indonesian state needs to be discussed. In the past, issues of decentralization have been discussed in a "region versus centre" or "Java versus outer Islands" framework. While it is true that Kalimantan is an "Outer Island", Amien Rais, first advocate of federalism, comes from Java and his party, while with strong support in Sumatra and elsewhere outside Java, also has a key support base on parts of the island of Java. The support for federalism in East Kalimantan has no real connection to identity or any aspect of geo-ethnic definition. Neither did any of Rais's justifications for federalism, nor later arguments favour decentralization.

The new situation that has arisen and continues to evolve does not pit outer regions against the centre but localism against national perspective. This is also consistent with the demands for decentralization which developed after 1999 from *kabupaten* and municipalities on the island of Java itself, even resulting in *kabupaten* splitting to form new ones. It reflects developments of contradictions more radical than those represented by the old region-versus-centre tensions. To the extent that some of the regional elites campaign for federalism or independence, and for greater and greater decentralization reflects a lack of interest among them in any perspective on national political or economic development. Federalists presented arguments that a federal state would not lead to a break-up of Indonesia. However, a break-up into several separate states is not the danger that is threatened by contemporary developments. It is rather a stagnation or disintegration of function of the national economy and political processes. Such a dysfunction, stagnation or disintegration relates not so much to the running of day-to-day state functions, but to solving national problems and fostering national development. There is a tension between national and local perspectives, embodied in the absence of a capacity to coordinate to achieve evenness among the country's heterogeneity and in the ideology of local ownership or priority of access to natural resources. These reflect a degeneration of national perspectives for development and progress into interest group localism. This has, of course, been enhanced by the process of "local capture" of district government by the politically leading local, smaller capitalists in many locations. In some ways, it is also a reflection of the same self-centred perspective on economic growth that develops among cronies under crony capitalism. A crony's fiefdom also has a sense of being "turf" to be protected and enhanced in the same way as a *kabupaten* or municipality might be seen as "turf" to the local elite.

A shift from centre against regions or outer against inner to national vis-à-vis local is a major and fundamental change in Indonesian politics and economy, with many ramifications. The former relates to the dynamics of a newly independent nation forged through an anti-colonial struggle which itself produced a new national culture, economy and polity but one which did not find a settled form and content immediately. Tensions and conflicts develop with those communities and polities that existed prior to the new nation formation process. A centre against regions or an inner (Java) versus outer tension is an inevitable part of a nation creation process, where that process has to deal with such pre-existing communities and polities. It can be handled well or poorly and can also be intervened in by external forces to negative effect. But it is a more or less normal phenomenon in all nation formation processes where pre-existing communities have existed.

This dynamic, very evident in the period immediately after independence — also explains the central importance of the state slogan: "Unity in Diversity". However, today fewer and fewer *kabupaten* and provinces articulate their complaints to the national government as complaints about the suppression of diversity (i.e. on ethnic grounds). In a province like East Kalimantan, ethnic identity vis-à-vis a centre or other ethnic identity becomes completely irrelevant.[89] When there is a grievance with the national level of government, it is now primarily over access to financial resources for local elites and the local government they have "captured". The same also applies when there are disputes between neighbouring districts. Even disputes such as that between East Kalimantan and the national level over the level of reimbursement to the province of revenues from national resources exploitation is actually a dispute with other provinces as all regions receive a legislated proportion of net domestic revenue. A rhetoric that discusses these issues in terms of region versus centre is misleading; the real issue is how wealth is dispersed nationally to facilitate national economic and social development.

The national–local perspectives tension that is visible in Indonesia today is a different phenomenon from that which occurred in the 1950s. A tension which can be perceived as being with/against "the centre" has spread throughout the country, including on (so-called inner) Java itself.[90] In fact, neither is it a matter of something spreading from outer to inner. Rather, it is the emergence of a new phenomenon throughout the country: the local could not care less about national needs. Rather than the early part of a nation creation process (as in the 1950s), the current processes represent a later failure of nation consolidation, rooted in the stunted development of classes and based on stunted economic development.

Class and National Agency

I have already presented the basic points of the argument that decentralization is a reflection of the severe weakening of conglomerate (former crony) political power, which was protected by a centralistic regime. This weakening is allowing greater initiative for local, small and medium capital, which still operates on a low level and small-scale.[91] Centralization under these conditions lacks national political agency. National scale development initiatives are minimal. There is neither national ideological direction, nor a national debate over development ideologies. There is no national conceptualization of how to deal with the "heterogeneity" and "factor immobility" that Pepinsky and Wihardja identify, which is with the very obvious uneven natural, economic and social (under)development of the country. Planning becomes tokenistic — also in synergy with contemporary international financial power's neo-liberal preferences.

I would like to conclude this essay with a brief discussion of trends that may represent developments responding to this vacuum of political agency with national perspective. After a hundred years of processes, there is an Indonesian nation, a historically created stable community living within established borders and with common language, psychology/culture and economic life, however unevenly developed. There had previously been a successfully powerful ruling class, or rather faction of a class, under Suharto and his crony capitalists. The embryo of this Suharto faction, a formation of armed capitalists in de facto control of national enterprises and army businesses between 1956 and 1965, grew during 1965 and 1998. While it was still in embryonic formation, before 1965, it and the then village elites were almost deposed as the ruling class by the rapidly growing peasant and worker movement organized by the PKI and ideologically co-led by Sukarno. This was a movement with very much a spreading national scale and national perspective. In fact, both sides of this pre-1965 struggle were led by core social forces and political leaderships with a national perspective. The post-65 physical elimination, banning and memory erasure of the pre-1965 peasant and worker movements and of socialist ideology destroyed the role of these classes and their leaderships. In terms of being a political agency, Indonesia was left with only a small, undeveloped, culturally weak embryonic social class faction — bureaucratic or military capitalists. It evolved into a faction of crony capitalists in the 1980s and 1990s, still protected by but separate from the military as an institution. The loss of this protection ended its status as cronies, eventually pitting them against each other. Weakened in these ways, it has lost most of its national-directing power. Its ideological justification via the ideology of "development" had also collapsed after the 1997 Asian financial crisis and Indonesia's economic turmoil. And, in any case, it was forbidden to the vast mass of the population to be actual participants in ideological life so even this ideology had never been deeply implanted at the grass roots.

The question must then be asked if there are any other processes occurring, even if at an early stage of development, that might indicate new formations of social forces that could rise to effective political agency, especially political agency that has national scale and perspectives. This question is also relevant in terms of agency as a pressure for accountability within the new electoral and representative processes connected with decentralization. There are two phenomena that need to be discussed at this point. First is the insertion into national politics of figures from local politics, creations of *desentralisasi*. The most significant of such insertions is that manifested in the rise of former mayor of Solo, Joko Widodo, to become Governor of Jakarta and a very possible President of Indonesia in 2014. The second is organized labour.[92]

Widodo emerges out of the locally based capitalist class in the town of Solo.

Local Capital as National Political Agency

The question is whether the increasing popularity of Joko Widodo, at least as manifested in polls and media support, represents something beyond the coincidental popularity of a special figure. Is there a process underway whereby local capital, or at least sections of it, are seeking a national presence through electoral politics, either as and for themselves, or as part of a wider alliance? A recognition of a realistic prospect of Widodo being nominated by the PDI-P as 2014 presidential candidate has only emerged in 2013, so whatever process is underway, it would appear to be at an early stage. As mentioned earlier in this essay, Widodo's deputy governor in Jakarta, Ahok, was also a *bupati* before he became a member of the national parliament and then deputy governor. Other local political figures such as Tri Rismaharini, mayor of Surabaya as well as Ganjar Pranowo, elected as Governor of Central Java in 2013, are also increasingly spoken of as potential national political leaders. Rismaharini has even been mentioned as a possible vice-presidential candidate alongside former Lieutenant General Prabowo, currently touted as presidential candidate for Gerindra. American supporters[93] of Prabowo, such as Stanley Weiss, Founding Chairman, Business Executives for National Security, recently wrote:

> There is also a potential running mate who would ideally complement Prabowo's discipline with a proven ability to achieve tangible, transformative results on the ground: Ibu Risma, mayor of Surabaya, Indonesia's second largest city. Recognized nationally as a reformer, praised by popular Jakarta Governor Joko Widodo for her relentless dedication to improving the lives of average Indonesians, the woman known as "Mother Risma" also has a strong anti-corruption record. She was the driving force in establishing Surabaya as the first city in Indonesia to implement a transparent e-government online system that reduced both costs and graft. There isn't another public figure in Indonesia, including Joko, who has a more sparkling record of achievement than the deeply humble Ibu Risma.[94]

As of September 2013, however, it is Widodo's insertion into national politics that is clearly the more significant. Widodo first stood for mayor in 2005 in Solo, Central Java. He had initially been in contact with the Islamic political groupings in Solo but eventually aligned with the PDI-P as he stepped forward to become a mayoral candidate. The Solo branch of the local

PDI-P had been through a crisis of leadership and had no popular potential candidates. Widodo was a prominent businessman, also holding the position of chairperson of the Solo businessmen's association. He was elected as the mayor in 2005 with 35.5 per cent of votes.[95] Four years later, in 2009, he won an extraordinary 91 per cent of votes in an election unmarred by repression of reports of cheating. His popularity was due to an increase in social safety net expenditure of various kinds, made possible by the extraordinary increase in the transfer of decentralization funds from the national government. In addition to this emphasis on social safety net policies, he also organized some renovations in traditional markets. Although only a tiny percentage of the population work in these traditional markets, the dilapidated state of their buildings is often seen as proof of indifference by elite-centred local governments to the needs of local people.

He also worked to streamline some bureaucratic procedures, especially to make them more accessible for Solo's small- and medium-sized businesses.

He combined these rather modest policies with a political style that stands in direct opposition to the style that has been adopted by almost all politicians since 1998. Even as electoral competition intensified after 1999, especially with the plethora of local elections, politicians continued to present themselves in the style of the authoritative and patriarchal New Order governmental official or *pejabat*. This style involved asserting a formal and patriarchal distance between politician and community. Politicians competed to look formal. After election, huge billboards would appear with their pictures, often wearing uniforms. Widodo adopted a style of often wearing casual clothes and making a habit of visiting poor hamlets, market places and street peddlers. He opened the mayoral buildings to use by community groups and NGOs. He incorporated community development NGOs into aspects of the decision-making process on some issues. He banned billboards of his picture (although he is never far from a media camera).

He was mayor during a period of revenue boom for Solo, as a result of the transfer of funds from the national government. Under that circumstance, and with the combination of policies described above, he was still very popular at the end of his term in Solo, when he began campaigning for the position of Governor of Jakarta. Now, he is presidential candidate for the PDI-P in 2014. He is topping all polls being held by the various political polling centres in Indonesia, including poll surveys covering all the country's provinces.

The question arises as to whether he appears to represent any deeper process that might be producing a social force capable of acting as a national political agency. Without such a social force-based political agency, even if he wins the Presidency, he will still be presiding over a parliament made up of several parties, all of whom are tied to either ex-crony, big capital or expanding local dynasties (or both) in a decentralized representative and administrative structure. A social force-based political agency implies the ability, in one form or other, to mobilize "civil society", i.e., different sectors of the population, as a pressure point on government, local and national. As a political agency that can encourage a coordinative approach, that social force mobilization capacity needs to have a national scale and perspective. Are there any signs that he is part of any process such as that?

Widodo is not the leader of any kind of social movement or political protest movement. Indeed, according to researchers working on his time in Solo, Widodo also spent no time on building or strengthening the PDI-P as a mobilizing party. Widodo's orientation is to electoral activity: winning votes. In many ways, his perspective on these issues is aimed at demobilizing, at convincing people that he has their interests at heart and that therefore they do not need to mobilize. His orientation to organized and mobilized communities in Jakarta has also been troubled, although not reported in the media.[96] While he signed formal political contracts with squatters in some *kampung* such as Pluit, promising them legal title, he has already moved to remove them from that same area.[97] There are absolutely no signs of Widodo emerging as a mobilizer of "civil society" for political activity. His tactic is to present himself as a listening patron, showing some generosity, so that the poor (as clients) will feel they must give up their protests, otherwise they would be ungrateful. He manipulates the elements of patron–client political culture that make poor client classes feel *"tidak tega"* ("feel bad") to oppose patron figures.

Is he though a symptom of some underlying process that may produce a new political agency, even if not consciously leading it himself? While I do not think there is enough evidence yet to be clear on this question, there are a few signs that are worth noting.

First, it has to be noted that Widodo's emergence on the scene as a possible PDI-P presidential candidate is giving a national political manifestation to the cleavage between the political parties of the ex-cronies and their allies. It is interesting that most of the high-profile big capitalists that aligned with the PDI-P in the late 1990s, such as Arifin Panigoro and Laksamana Sukardi, have dropped away from the PDI-P. During the whole period of the Yudhoyono government, the PDI-P has not been a part of the ruling coalition, which has contained Aburizal Bakrie's Golkar, and the Democratic Party, which includes multimillionaire conglomerate figure Dahlan Iskan. The Prosperous Justice Party (PKS) has been tarnished with cronyism as a result of partnering the national leadership. Also, its cabinet minister was embroiled in a major corruption scandal. In many respects the PDI-P presents itself as the party without crony or big conglomerate connections. However, until very recently, it was having difficulty in defining itself even at the level of rhetorical profile. There has been its association with Joko Widodo, and also Risma in Surabaya, and Ganjar Pranowo, the new governor in Central Java. All these have begun to provide it with the material to develop a stronger profile. PDI-P chairperson Megawati has toured Widodo like a mascot around Indonesia, presenting him as an example of the new kind of "cadre" that the PDI-P wants to develop. PDI-P candidates have taken to adopting his checkered shirt during local election campaigns.

Decentralization has, on the one hand, facilitated local capture by business elites and the spread of corruption. On the other hand, it has also opened up the possibility of what might be called "social safety net populism". *Kabupaten* and municipal government has become the level of government that provides and is seen to provide basic services and social safety net provisions, such as free health care and education cards for those registered as poor, i.e., the poorest of the poor. Armed with the considerable increase in revenue transfers to local government, it has been possible for a handful of such figures to develop high levels of popularity based on perceptions of improved service provision, even where it has been very modest. These very modest changes contrast favourably with those other local government performances where corrupt family fiefdoms have captured local government. Such figures are also not creatures of the upper levels of Jakarta's surreal world of the super-wealthy, far removed from any normal communications with people from other layers of society.

Representatives of centralistic conglomerate interests outside of the ruling coalition, such as Prabowo and Gerindra, have also become increasingly hostile to Widodo. Gerindra persistently issued statements that Widodo should postpone thinking of presidential candidacy until 2019. Prabowo increasingly attacks the favourable media coverage that Widodo has been receiving.

Widodo may indeed represent an early manifestation of a national political leadership starting to emerge out of the realm of district level business and politics. Others, such as Risma and Ganjar, and perhaps Ahok, may follow. If this is what is happening, however, such a leadership will need to come up with a more developed ideological and policy package than one comprising simply of symbolic acts to enhance their positions as "good patrons" and very limited social safety net and administrative improvements. To become a party that would facilitate national co-ordination capacity, they would need a national economic perspective (and even a plan) based on trying to level the country's resource unevenness as part of a national development strategy. Their ideology would have to convince enough of society to mobilize politically in order to defeat the elites in resource rich regions. Most difficult of all, they would have to forge some consensus among the 500 district elites, or at least a significant portion of them, behind such an ideology and perspective.

The main vehicle for building such a political agency capacity at this point would be the PDI-P. It is difficult to assess the state of the PDI-P throughout the country and at the district level. One indication, however, of the focus on reformulating an ideological and strategic package that could provide the basis for a new generation of party leadership building the party into an effective national political agency for its specific programme is its recent National Working Meeting (RAKERNAS) held in September, 2013. The RAKERNAS is an important mechanism of the PDI-P for the formulation of its strategies. This particular RAKERNAS was essentially important for two reasons. First, it was the first of such RAKERNAS preparing the PDI-P's campaign approach for the 2014 elections campaigns. Second, it took place in an atmosphere of heightened interest in the candidature of Widodo for the presidency in 2014. While the RAKERNAS made no decision on the candidacy, authorizing Megawati Sukarnoputri to make a decision at the appropriate time, there were no shortage of photo opportunities of Megawati seated with Widodo. Photographs of other local government PDI-P leaders attending the conference were also prominent.

The RAKERNAS came out with a list of seventeen "Recommendations". This package of recommendations provides a platform for the function that the PDI-P has claimed for itself, as an "opposition", although within the general framework of Indonesian capitalism. It starts to flesh out a programme that a party leadership, drawing on the social safety net populist local leaders, may be able to use to build a national electoral coalition that would be an effective alternative to the conglomerate-based parties. The seventeen recommendations include a series of statements in support of several very general statements in support of basic New Order and post-New Order symbols: Pancasila, the 1945 Constitution, the concept of the unitary republic as well as the state slogan of "Unity in Diversity". There are various other general statements picking up what are seen to be failures by the Yudhoyono government in solving economic and service provision issues as one would expect of an opposition party in a normal parliamentary system.

There are some points worth noting, however, that have implications for potential political agency. First is the call for:

Returning to the People's Consultative Assembly (MPR) the authority to plan, formulate and implement the broad outlines of comprehensive, planned national development. (Recommendation no. 3)[98]

The MPR, as it is presently constituted, comprises the members of the House of Representatives as well as the regional representatives that make up the newly formed Regional Representatives Council (DPD). The authorization of the MPR, including these regional representatives, would at least provide a national forum in which questions of interaction and interrelations between regions and the uneven development of the country could be discussed in the context of formulating national development policy. Of course, such a reform would remain an institutional reform and would not in and of itself overcome the reality of the political economy that I have discussed in this essay. A forum remains simply a forum while there is no political agency capable of ensuring that any "broad outlines" would actually be implemented on the ground. Such outlines would remain as much at the mercy of the realities of the map of class power as the technocratic dreams that Hadiz critiqued in *Localizing Power*. As a political statement, however, it stands in contrast to the practice of the last decade where the MPR, and thus the regional-based DPD also, had a reduced role, even as a discussion forum, in discussing national priorities. There has been no such national discussion anywhere.

The second aspect of the seventeen recommendations worthy of note in terms of potential political agency is the support for policies that have become important precisely because of the recent more effective role of class-based mobilizations. It has two recommendations that can be directly related to gains made by the increasingly active trade union movement. The first relates to wages and outsourcing:

> A struggle for a Wages Law that considers wage levels based on surveys of dignified living levels (*hidup layak*) aimed also at reducing the gap between highest paid and lowest wages.

Although formulated broadly and easily capable of reinterpretation later, this demand is relatively consistent with the campaigns of trade unions which have mobilized in very large numbers in 2012 and 2013. Furthermore, the emphasis on determining wages based on surveys of *hidup layak* standards stands in direct contradiction to the perspectives articulated by the representatives of conglomerate capital, and the current government. Sofyan Wanandi is listed no. 80 by *Globe Asia* in its list of 150 of Indonesia's richest. He is a classic crony, having been close to the Suharto clique at the very beginning of the New Order. He is now the chairperson of the Indonesian Businessmen's Association (APINDO). APINDO has fought against all the recent wage increases won by the trade unions, successfully getting the Yudhoyono government to approve postponements from paying the increases to hundreds of companies. Taking propaganda advantage of the recent drop in the foreign exchange value of the rupiah, Wanandi has also successfully campaigned for the government to adopt a position against allowing repeats of 2012 and 2013 wage increases. More specifically Wanandi has opposed the determination of wages based on calculations of *hidup layak* standards. As recently as 26 September 2013, at almost the same time as the PDI-P RAKERNAS, he stated:

> Up until now [when determining wages] the only consideration has been the *hidup layak* standards for workers. There has not been consideration of productivity levels in Indonesia compared with other countries. Even worse, the demands for *hidup layak* wage rises have been sought through demonstrations and not negotiations.[99]

The RAKERNAS also approved a recommendation supporting the new laws providing for a National Social Security System, including the 2011 law establishing the Social Security Implementation Body. The RAKERNAS decision also called for the government to begin full implementation starting January 2014. Again, the recommendations are formulated in ways that would be easy to wiggle out of once in power. However, this Law, like the recent wage rises, was won partly as a result of large scale mobilizations and ongoing campaigns by the biggest trade unions, which have been active over the last three years.

The recommendations also included promises to campaign for increased nursing facilities, at the local level and more funding for social services and education.

At least on paper, these recommendations may provide a platform that both encompasses increasing the role of national co-ordination among regions through an enhanced role for the MPR (which includes the DPD) and policies that link up with the ongoing campaigns of the most organized and mobilized section of "civil society" (the non-capitalist classes), namely the trade unions. The point here is not to make an assessment of whether the PDI-P is either capable or genuine or has a perspective that can actually solve Indonesia's major problems of underdevelopment, corruption and inequalities. The question is whether such a platform, drawing on figures coming out of the district capitalist class, such as Widodo, can become an organization capable of *at least testing out its capacity for civil society mobilization and the fostering of national coordination*. Such a test case would also be a challenge to the conglomerate-based political groupings.

Whether such a test case actually evolves will not be something that can be decided by the PDI-P leadership in isolation from other developments impacting on potentialities for political agency. As mentioned above, the PDI-P has adopted, however softly articulated, some positions consistent with the trade union campaigns of 2012 and 2013. These campaigns were not politically radical and called only for wage rises, a curtailing in the use of labour hire and for a national social insurance scheme, although they were resisted ferociously by APINDO and the government. They did however mobilize hundreds of thousands of people. At least one PDI-P member of parliament, Rieke Diah Pitaloka, was an active campaigner in support of the trade union campaigns. She both lobbied in parliament for the reforms as well as encouraged and participated in the large protest mobilizations organized by the trade unions. She was, however, the only PDI-P MP to do so. Her approach in encouraging mobilizations appears in contrast to the political approach of Joko Widodo whose aim is to discourage mobilizations in favour of surrendering problem resolution to the listening patron. Insofar as Pitaloka is the only PDI-P MP who has taken this stance, perhaps the prognosis for the PDI-P evolving as an active, mobilizing political agency is not good.[100]

Labour and Agency

In terms of any competition between these different perspectives in the PDI-P, and outside it, the actual developments in the labour movement are noteworthy. While the key features are the developments since the fall of Suharto, we must always also bear in mind the fact that historically, it was the peasantry and working class that provided the backbone and class basis for the national political movement that grew rapidly between the 1950s and 1965, achieving an active support base of around 20 million people. The first priority of the New Order government was to destroy this movement and eliminate any memory of it from political life.

Hadiz, back before 2007, in his book *Localizing Power* also recognized the importance of assessing labour's possible role in democratization and decentralization. He spent some time looking at labour. Hadiz's perspective, however, is inhibited by the "theoretical" starting point for his analysis of decentralization, and his general analysis of Indonesian politics, namely that Indonesia is in the period of the rise of capital. Forces outside the capitalist class are inevitably marginalized for the foreseeable future. This is consistent with Aspinall's description of contemporary political analysis on Indonesian politics, including Hadiz's, as exhibiting "the absence in their analysis of ... the transformative potential of subordinated groups".[101] Of course, the extent to which "subordinated groups" — in this case labour, the majority of the population — can exert influence on politics may be either weak or great at any specific time and place. Any analysis of labour politics, however, especially assessing its role in the democratization processes, as Hadiz frames his analysis, needs to seek to identify processes and trends, not just take snapshots of momentary situations. Such a snapshot approach robs the reality of process and can often create a blindness on the possibilities of change. Hadiz reviews the state of the trade unions in 2005 when he researched for the book.[102] The one major empirical weakness of this section is the total absence of any review of the developments that had already begun very soon after 1999 within the old state-backed trade union, the Serikat Pekerja Seluruh Indonesia (SPSI or All Indonesia Workers' Union). After 2000, when the state stepped back from direct hands-on control over the SPSI, a process of break-up and re-forming began eventually producing union formations, some of which have been able to wage campaigns of steadily increasing, even if still limited, influence. As a consequence, and reflecting also his theoretical prejudices, there is no identification of the trends which have led to this contemporary situation. In fact, Hadiz asserts that the situation in 2005 was "exactly the case as before Suharto's fall". Hadiz writes:

Apart from some well-coordinated mass mobilisations, notably those conducted on Labour Day 1 May, cross-class alliances involving labour continue to be restricted to small segments of middle-class-based NGOs and student movements. This was exactly the case before Soeharto's fall (Tornquist 2002).[103] There are also few overt signs of sufficiently coherent working-class organising, or social alliances that prominently include workers, which would seriously trouble local elites and governments anywhere.[104]

This analysis was easier to arrive at, given the absence of any investigation on the processes inside or around the SPSI.

His concluding summary on the role of labour identifies no trends that bring change in any form, but rather has a very solid sense of finality about it:

Thus, several major factors have combined to ensure the continuing marginalisation of labour in the post-authoritarian era and to inhibit its capacity to engage in local arenas of political conflict. First is the legacy of authoritarian rule, which was particularly harsh on organised labour in the first place — circumventing workers' organisational capacities through systematic, and often brutal, state repression. Quite simply, organised labour has not been able to overcome this legacy and re-learn the skills of effective organising and perhaps still needs to reclaim the tradition of political unionism that was so much a part of labour history before the New Order (Hadiz 1997, chapter 3). Second, the context of chronic massive unemployment and underemployment, especially in the wake of the economic crisis of 1997 and 1998, which Indonesia still struggles to overcome, is not particularly conducive to effective labour-organising efforts, even when their ambitions are confined to the local level only. Third, national and local elites continue to have political and ideological dispositions that are broadly anti-labour, which can be explained on the basis of their political socialisation and backgrounds in New Order-nurtured social organisations.[105]

The PDI-P's adoption of a position on wages and on social security is a recognition of the ability of labour to have an impact on national politics. In order to assess the trends in this arena and its potential for national political agency, it is necessary to briefly review the most recent developments in the labour movement.

In its press statement on 3 October 2013, the Indonesian Workers and Labourers Assembly (MPBI) stated that 2 million workers mobilized for the national strike it called for that date, with mobilizations in industrial areas or outside government offices in twenty-one cities and towns.[106] The MPBI comprised several of the major trade union confederations that had evolved out of the old SPSI after splits and re-formations as well as a growing spread in organizing capacity. Press and various blog reports separately estimate hundreds of thousands of workers mobilized in Jakarta's various industrial estate areas, gathering at many different rally points. It is reported that tens of thousands of others gathered in Indonesia's larger cities and thousands in smaller towns. The strike was scheduled to go for a few more days but the MPBI leadership called it off after one day, following another round of meetings with President Yudhoyono's Minister for Labour. The demands articulated by the MPBI, and supported by other unions outside this formation, including the more overtly left-wing, but much smaller, Workers Secretariat, were for an increase in wages, and end to "outsourcing" and the full implementation of health insurance legislation which would guarantee coverage to all workers, with employers paying the premiums. This, of course, is linked to the PDI-P's later RAKERNAS recommendation.

However many workers exactly mobilized, the strike marked a clear turning point in the shaping of the political terrain for the mobilization of "civil society" in popular struggle. Labour, even if still only a miniscule portion of the workforce is organized, has entered onto the political stage, and this entrance is based on the increased self-confidence and combativeness of workers, especially in the industrial estate areas. These areas, where factories are jammed in beside each other and tens of thousands of workers swarm to their workplaces every morning, have been the centre of labour militancy since the 1990s, when still under the Suharto dictatorship. In the 1990s, garment, footwear and textile workers played a leading role. Now workers in the large plants assembling cars, motorbikes and white goods are playing a leading role. As these sectors "boom", the bargaining position of the unions, which have reorganized in the more liberal atmosphere since the fall of Suharto, is providing the material base for the increased self-confidence. However, such a boost in confidence — and combativity — cannot be a simple mechanistic product of the new political economy of manufacturing.

Among labour solidarity activists, there are different reasons given to explain the origins of what they term *"radikalisasi"* — I think, better described as increased combativity. These are: the inspiration from a long strike by workers at the Freeport mine in West Papua for better wages which achieved positive outcomes although other activists think the strikes across Java have been more important in inspiring combativeness; the success of the campaign by the Social Security Action Committee (KASJ), a coalition of NGOs and unions, in winning health insurance legislation in 2011, and the success of the protest movement in

May 2012 which succeeded in forcing the government to delay an increase in petrol and kerosene prices. Union-led worker mobilizations were crucial to all these campaigns.

It is clear also that conscious propagandizing for more militant and solidarizing activities among the workers and careful tactical planning have also been crucial in this process — preceding even the Freeport strike. This education and planning seem to have been initiated from within the Federation of Indonesian Metal Workers' Unions (FSPMI).[107] An article entitled "Rachmat, Tarikh (Sejarah), Hidayah dan Rekomendasi"[108] (Positive Results of the Struggle: History, Lessons and Recommendations), by Danial Indrakusuma in *Majalah Sedane* throws some light on these processes.[109]

In this article, Indrakusuma explains the factors that he thinks have led to the increased workers' self-confidence. In some ways, he echoes the three points above, but also points to the internal processes inside the FPSMI and other unions. Among these were the workers involvement in research and seminar activities carried out in conjunction with research-oriented NGOs. This deepened workers' understanding of the wage system and, more crucially, the extent of "outsourcing" and the gap between the current outsourcing situation and existing legislation. According to Indrakusuma, almost 80 per cent of workers carrying out central work in the country's major plants were "outsourced" workers, i.e., workers with basically a casual status. Outsourcing, it was revealed, was not a "supplementary" form of employment but the situation of the vast majority of the factory workforce. This, says Indrakusuma, has been the basis for the successful *"gerunduk"* tactic where workers from one or more factories will rally outside other factories calling on those inside also to stop work. The fact that almost all the workers everywhere are casual and have an interest in opposing "outsourcing" provides the basis for practical solidarity. Solidarity actions between workers in different factories, and between unions, have forced some employers to transfer workers on to a permanent basis, as provided by law. Thousands of workers have achieved permanency. The law on outsourcing restricts it to only supplementary work and work of a temporary nature. The unions are opposing all kinds of outsourcing.

Indrakusuma's article also depicts a process where there has been a conscious attempt in improving the quality of mobilizations. The steps have included: encouragement of workers to attend the pickets and protests of other unions and factories; involvement in issues not directly related to the employer but to government and parliament, such as the social insurance law; and stop-works that spread through a whole industrial enclave and close it down. The most significant of these was the January 2012 stop-work and rally by 200,000 workers in several industrial enclaves on the eastern edge of Jakarta, in West Java province. There has also been, says Indrakusuma, a policy of encouraging *"rapat akbar"* (mass meetings, though the Indonesian term conjures up the vision of the great anti-colonial mass meetings before independence). These sessions discuss strategy and tactics as well as a means of showing support for demands on the government. The greatest success in this area was the 2012 May Day rally organized by the MPBI (at its forming) in the main Jakarta sports stadium, with at least 60,000 workers present. Indrakusuma also goes into detail on specific struggles in different factories that he considers have had an important impact.

The article also points to the confidence-building presence of the Garda Metal (Metal Guard), a disciplined formation of the more physically prepared workers who often lead mobilizations and provide a sense of security. There is always a strong police, and sometimes military, presence at demonstrations. The *rapat akbar* rallies, the mass stop-works, the mobilizations shutting down whole enclaves and the raising of the spectre of a political challenge to the government — the emergence of organized labour as an organized political actor — has important implications for the emergence of a "civil society" based political agency.

The political character of the new unions and the mass sentiment will also be crucial. Is there a developing challenge within all these processes to trade union consciousness, to create a new consciousness? Are there processes that point in the direction of a greater consciousness among the worker sector regarding "political agency". Although Indrakusuma does not use this term, he addresses this issue positively:

> The most important political consciousness that has grown alongside all these struggles is that these affairs of labour cannot be resolved outside of politics, outside of the struggle for power. It is that consciousness which pushes us to control the state. The other important political consciousness that has grown is that workers (*buruh*/labourers) must be the vanguard in the struggle for the interest of the [whole] people, not just for the workers, especially as we need the votes of the people in elections as well as their political support (in the sense of mass support).

The fact that the Yudhoyono government resumed negotiations with MPBI leaders on the day of the strike indicated it was sensitive to the threat that any ongoing worker protest momentum represents, especially to immediate commercial interests. APINDO and other employer groups in the lead-up to and on the day of the strike protested strongly. While editorials were often hostile to the strike, working journalists' reports were generally sympathetic. The Minister for Economic Affairs, Hatta Rajasa, came out of the strike apparently supporting the wage increase being asked for by the unions (from about the current US$200 per month to around US$250).

The October mobilizations were demanding increases in the official minimum wage. Interestingly reinforcing some of the decentralization-related dynamics, minimum wage increases are decided at the *kabupaten* and municipality level after the deliberations of a tripartite wage board which surveys *hidup layak* needs. The wage board recommendations are then acted upon by the *bupati* or *walikota*. In the immediate weeks after the October protests, rises in the minimum wages were confirmed by *bupati*, mayors and, in Jakarta's case by the Governor, of between 40 and 70 per cent. No doubt these *bupati* and mayors were also calculating the electoral advantages and disadvantages of any position they took on this issue, especially in districts where factories were congregated and unions active, such as in the Kerawang and Bekasi areas. Certainly these unions were not feeling that they were experiencing the "continuing marginalization of labour" that Hadiz had discussed in 2010.

During 2013, however, the trade unions suffered a long series of disappointments. APINDO successfully lobbied for many companies to have their duty to pay the new minimum wage postponed. There was a serious counter-offensive against the trade unions.[110] One Indonesian union solidarity activist and trade union journalist, Sherr Rinn, has written on these developments:

> There was an immediate counterattack. Anti-worker leaflets threatening strikers in the name of various new organisations appeared among communities in the poor factory worker areas. Soon after, gangs of thugs appeared, sometimes up to 400 men, recruited from the poorest areas.
>
> They attacked and harassed picket lines and burned down worker offices. Many companies started to deploy these thugs, as well as soldiers, on site. The thugs would follow outspoken workers home and threaten them and their families.

Meanwhile, when companies had been forced to end labour hire, they would upgrade workers to contracts, but often give different groups better or worse conditions, dividing the union membership. Some workers have been charged with criminal libel against employers and may end up in court or jail.

In other cases, workers were made redundant and offered pay-offs, resulting in drops in memberships of some unions. Many employers have successfully applied to government bodies for a postponement of wage rises. Despite inspiring incidents of workers fighting off large brigades of thugs back in November, there has been a demoralising impact on sections of the union membership.

This has been made worse by union bureaucrat conservatism. Almost immediately after the counterattack started, there were retreats. On 8 November, union leaders, including from the FSPMI, signed a "Declaration of Harmony" with APINDO and government officials.

In the aftermath of this agreement, union leaderships discouraged worker protests, including the popular solidarity actions between factories. Workers were instructed to withdraw from several union-community alliances in several cities.[111]

When writing this in August, 2013 she assessed:

The counter-offensive has been successful in damping worker activity; strikes and other protests have been in decline since around November. In recent talks with the minister of industry and the head of the Indonesian Entrepreneurs Association (APINDO), the heads of two major union federations more or less offered support for the government's insistence that unions exercise wage restraint.

However, this was rejected by another leader, Said Iqbal, from the Indonesian Metal Workers Federation (FSPMI), who is also head of the major union alliance Indonesian Workers Assembly (MPBI), which organised the 3 October mobilization. The other union leaders were also members of MPBI, indicating that new differences might be emerging among the union leaders.

By September 2013, it had become clearer that the trend towards developing a potential to assert political agency has in fact grown. While on the one hand, the MPBI appears to quietly go into limbo, a new initiative emerged aimed at organizing another major mobilization for October 2013. A "Preparatory Committee for National Consolidation"[112] was formed combining the forces of the Indonesian Trade Union Confederation (KSPI), which includes the FSPMI,[113] with those of the left-wing (but very small) oriented union alliance Workers Secretariat (Sekber Buruh). This protest occurred on 31 October and 1 November, mobilizing tens of thousands of workers. It may have been smaller than the 2012 strike, given a lesser level of unity, with only one of the MPBI federations participating. There were also better planned harassment by anti-strike militia and thugs. The impact of the strike on the political atmosphere was less than in 2012, and governments offered much lower wage increases than previously. At the same time, however, there appeared to be more systematic attempts to lead the protests from the grass-roots — rather than from the union bureaucracy — using the technique of "sweeping" where workers who have gone out on strike go from factory to factory encouraging others to follow suit. Activists say that this resulted in a big increase in workers who actually went on strike as distinct from joining protests after or before their shift. Since December, there has been a string of follow-up actions by individual factories as well as an escalation in the level of organization by those at the base who are dissatisfied with the current leaderships.

Labour, Decentralization and National Political Agency

There can be little doubt that the new labour organizing and political activity represents a trend in a direction away from marginalization of this sector from both local and national politics. The winning of increases in the minimum wage, formalized at local government level, and the passing of a social insurance law in the national parliament are clear measures of this change. The ongoing efforts at reorganization, as alliances come and go, also indicate that this process is likely to be resilient, ongoing process, even if the final outcome is still unknown. One thing that is clear, however, is that the process will not remain within the limits of industrial or trade union activity.

While there are occasional whispers of a new party emerging — a socialist workers party — there are no visible moves in that direction yet. There are an increasing number of manifestations of union campaigning bursting beyond the narrow industrial framework. One example is the 2013 campaign for Governor of West Java run by PDI-P MP, Rieke Diah Pitaloka. Her support for the trade union mobilizations campaigning for the social insurance legislation and for wage rises has won her popularity among the factory worker population. She spoke at many union rallies as part of that campaign, as well as supporting wage campaigns. She (and the PDI-P) had a support base inside the FSPMI. During her campaign, there were several rallies that were made up of thousands of workers from the factory belt areas of West Java, outside of Jakarta, despite the trade union leaderships taking a formally neutral position. Pitaloka was defeated by candidates from an Islamic party, who had superior support from the rural areas. Pitaloka and some worker groups complained that thousands of workers were unable to vote because they were not allowed time off work to go to the voting booths. Pitaloka will now be standing for the PDI-P in the electoral district where there is a significant concentration of factory workers in the 2014 parliamentary elections. The PKS is also standing a candidate — a member of the FSPMI — revealing political differences between workers, as many continue to support Pitaloka. Said Iqbal, president of KSPI and FSPMI, is pressuring FSPMI members to support the PKS candidate. He himself is from a PKS background. Meanwhile it is rumoured that another key FSPMI leader, Obon Tabrani, has joined the PDI-P and it is also therefore expected that he will support Pitaloka.

Furthermore, it is now also very clear that there will be a direct intervention by the trade unions in the electoral process. The FSPMI has decided on a "Buruh Go Politik" (Workers Go Politics) campaign, intervening in elections at the local level, introduced through the decentralization process. The FSPMI has selected nine of its members to stand as candidates in elections for the parliaments for the Bekasi *kabupaten* and municipal parliaments as well as the West Java provincial parliaments. Initially the nine candidates were to be elected from within the FSPMI, but in the end, they were appointed by the FSPMI leadership. Successfully, they have had these nine candidates nominated by five different political parties, namely the PDI-P, PAN, PKS, PPP and the small Indonesia Unity and Justice Party (PKPI). Billboards with their work and union history have appeared throughout the Bekasi area. Apart from this initiative by the FSPMI itself, individual political parties are also recruiting prominent unionists to stand as candidates. The PKS, for example, will be standing an FSPMI unionist, Iswan Abdullah, as a candidate in the Karawang district.

He will be up against the PDI-P's Pitaloka, in terms of being a specific focus of worker support. Iswan is further down the PKS list than Pitaloka is on the PDI-P list — she is on top of the list. So the confrontation is not a direct one, but relates more to the loyalties and focus of FSPMI members.

In these circumstances, the trend for union mobilization to be further politicized will inevitably evolve further. There can be little doubt that this is the embryo of an already evolving political agency coming onto the scene. However, does this new process also contain an *anational*, localized political framework or is this labour sector evolving with a national perspective and scale? On this question, the process is also clear. All of the union confederations organize on a national scale. The October 2013 union protests involved coordinated actions with the same demands and schedules in at least twenty towns and cities. The most recent development — the formation of the Preparatory Committee for National Consolidation — emphasizes "national" in its name. The unions listed as invited come from sixteen regions from Aceh to Papua, and all points in between.[114] Unions still only organized at the regional level, as well as already nationally organized unions have been invited. The "Terms of Reference" document prepared for the national consolidation manifests a very strong consciousness about organizing nationally. In a section headed "Next steps by the workers of Indonesia" includes the following two (of four) points:

- Preparation of our next action which will take place in more than 200 of Indonesia's *kabupaten* and municipalities, including; Jakarta, Bogor, Bekasi, Depok, Subang, Karawang, Purwakarta, Bandung, Cimahi, Sukabumi, Tangerang, Serang, Cilegon, Cirebon, Cilacap, Pekalongan, Semarang, Kendal, Demak, Solo, Yogyakarta, Surabaya, Sidoarjo, Mojokerto,

Pasuruan, Batam, Bintan, Riau, Palembang, Medan, Deli Serdang, Banda Aceh, Lhokseumawe, Kuala Simpang, Lampung, Makassar, Gorontalo, Kaltim, Kalsel and other areas.

- The preparation of the national strike involving 5 million workers at the end of October 2013 in 20 provinces and 200 *kabupaten*/municipalities of Indonesia.

This strike, although not involving all the MPBI unions, and not reaching 5 million workers, did still achieve a national spread.

It might be added here that while it is impossible to predict with total certainty, electoral formations are likely to be crucial in the further evolution of class-based social agency. As cited in this essay, the Ministry of Labour claims approximately 3 million union members out of a workforce of more than 100 million. A very large proportion of that more than 100 million are part of the massive informal proletariat. Alliances between formal and informal proletariat in the pursuit of policies delivering improvements in material conditions and rights may very well, at least in the short-term, find a stable form in electoral formations, even though they may be ones that also carry out social movement type activities, that is, extra-parliamentary activity.

Conclusion

The post-Suharto political economy, i.e., post-cronyism, has facilitated a decentralization (introduced during a period of technocratic interregnum under President Habibie and supported by international donor forces) that is set in an *anational*, political framework. This reflects the absence of any strong national, class-based, political agency that can assert its agenda nationally — whatever that might be. A weakened layer of ex-crony conglomerate capital, no longer protected by the military-backed centralistic Suharto regime, lost its ability to assert a clear national agenda over the plethora of small and medium capitalists operating at a local level, who themselves do not operate on a national scale or have a clear national development perspective. This has accentuated the dysfunctional aspects of decentralization, both in terms of capture of local government and corruption as well as inability to deal with the unevenness/heterogeneity/factor immobility of the archipelago. This weakness also makes it easier for international capital to assert its interests in the formulation of national economic policy. The inadequacy — or in some cases, the complete inability to formulate solutions or identify potential "solutional" trends in the available literature — reflects the absence of a focus on the question of social class and political agency. I hope this essay

shows that an analysis which searches for trends that relate
to such an agency will yield more explanatory and interesting
results and point to the kind of further research agenda that
may be useful.

Endnotes

1. I would like to thank Dr Ian Wilson, Professor Olle Törnquist, Professor James Peacock and Associate Professor Toby Carroll for their input on this essay.
2. See Max Lane, *Unfinished Nation: Indonesia Before and After Suharto* (London and New York: Verso, 2008).
3. Edward Aspinall, "The Politics of Studying Indonesian Politics: Intellectuals, Political Research and Public Debate in Australia ", in *Knowing Indonesia: Intersections of Self, Discipline and Nation*, edited by Jemma Purdey (Clayton: Monash University Publishing, 2012). This chapter is also available online at <http://books.publishing. monash.edu/apps/bookworm/view/Knowing+Indonesia%3A+Int ersections+of+Self%2C+Discipline+and+Nation/177/OEBPS/c04. htm>. Aspinall in more recent writings has expressed that there is no need for "morbid pessimism" as improvements in welfare for the population have begun and will be felt eventually after a "multigenerational struggles over long time periods". Edward Aspinall, "Popular Agency and Interests in Indonesia's Democratic Transition and Consolidation", in *Indonesia*, No. 96, Special Issue: Wealth, Power, and Contemporary Indonesian Politics (October 2013), p. 121.
4. Vedi Hadiz, *Localising Power in Post-Authoritarian Indonesia: A Southeast Asia Perspective* (Stanford: Stanford University Press, 2010).
5. Vedi Hadiz and Richard Robison, *Reorganising Power in Indonesia: The Politics of Oligarchy in an Age of Markets*, (New York: Routledge, 2004), pp. 120–44; Hadiz, *Localising Power in Post-Authoritarian Indonesia*, pp. 145–57. Hadiz's commentary on labour and local politics is discussed further in the final section of this essay.

6. Widjajanti I. Suharyo, "Indonesia's Transition to Decentralised Governance: Evolution at the Local Level", in *Decentralization and Regional Autonomy in Indonesia: Implementation and Challenges*, edited by Coen J.G. Holtzappel and Martin Ramstedt (Singapore: Institute of Southeast Asian Studies and IIAS, 2009), p. 96.

7. Ibid.

8. Law No. 32/2004 on the Fiscal Balance of Regional Administration, available in *Decentralization and Regional Autonomy in Indonesia*, edited by Holtzappel and Ramstedt, pp. 49–51.

9. See Soetandya Wignusubroto et al., *Pasang Surut Otonomi Daerah Sketsa Perjalanan 100 Tahun* (Jakarta: Institute for Local Development and Yayasan TIFA, November 2005); Abdul Gaffar Karim, *Kompleksitas Persoalan Otonomi Daerah di Indonesia* (Jakarta: Jurusan Ilmu Pemerintahan, Universitas Gadjah Mada & Pustaka Pelajar, 2003); "Format Daerah Otonomi Indonesia (Laporan Akhir Penilitian)", Ilmu Pemerintahan, Universitas Gadjah Mada, 1997.

10. "Form a council of political leaders to safeguard the sovereignty of the people!", National Committee for Democratic Struggle, January 1998.

11. PIJAR's Tritura 1998, Posted by Tapol, 11 January 1998.

12. "VISI calon presiden RI", 26 February 1998, 23:56:56 PST, <http://www.library.ohiou.edu/indopubs/1998/02/28/0076.html>.

"ada sejumlah agenda yang sudah selalu siap dalam kepala saya. Pertama, seluruh kekayaan alam, baik di hutan-hutan maupun di gunung-gunung dan di perut bumi berupa hasil pertambangan harus diselamatkan untuk anak cucu kita sendiri. Yang sekarang ini, saya yakin ada mismanagement yang sangat fatal di dalam mengelola hutan tropis, kekayaan tambang yang bersifat migas, apalagi yang non-migas. Kedua, pemerintah yang bersih harus mulai ditegakkan dengan cara bertahap, dengan jalan menanggulangi dua penyakit kembar yang sudah kronis yaitu korupsi dan kolusi. Ketiga, harus diupayakan seoptimal mungkin pengurangan jarak yang sekarang kian melebar antara kaum the have dan kaum the have not. Kesenjangan sosial ini harus ditutup secara bertahap dan sistematik. Keempat, Bhineka Tunggal Ika sebagai rahasia kekuatan bangsa harus dipegang teguh dan tidak boleh sedikit pun diusik, mengingat sekali ada langkah mengusik *Bhinneka Tunggal Ika*, maka

Indonesia sebagai sebuah negara dan bangsa akan berada dalam bahaya. Kelima, perlu adanya koalisi besar dan bersih dari ABRI (TNI AD), Golkar, partai-partai, ormas, kampus, pengusaha, LSM dan lain-lain yang masih belum terlalu jauh kena polusi korupsi dan kolusi. Koalisi besar dan bersih inilah yang diharapkan dapat memikul tugas-tugas nasional pada masa mendatang. Dan akhirnya tentu perubahan-perubahan yang bersifat reformatif harus diambil selangkah demi selangkah sehingga tidak perlu mengagetkan karena kebijaksanaan-kebijaksanaan yang radikal dan dramatis akan memperparah keadaan ..."

13. Ibid. "Kita harus menciptakan pemerintah yang bersih dan berwibawa, yaitu:
    1. Pemerintah yang mampu mengambil kebijaksanaan yang sesuai dengan Amanat Penderitaan Rakyat;
    2. Pemerintah yang para pejabatnya tidak terlibat dalam kegiatan usaha memperkaya diri melalui kolusi, korupsi dan nepotisme;
    3. Pemerintah yang dapat dan mau dikontrol oleh hukum dan rakyatnya melalui lembaga demokrasi dan lembaga peradilan."

14. Ibid.

15. It can be noted that the electoral turnout was weak in areas of Megawati supporters as she advocated an election boycott. This was, however, a very passive boycott. It represented a failure on the part of the incumbent political controllers, not a rebellion or sabotage by them.

16. John Sidel, "Bossism and democracy in the Philippines, Thailand, and Indonesia: Towards an alternative framework for the study of 'local strongmen'", in *Politicising Democracy: The New Local Politics of Democratisation*, edited by John Harriss, Kristin Stokke and Olle Törnquist (International Political Economy Series) (Basingstoke: Palgrave Macmillan, 2004), pp. 51–74.

17. Coen J.G. Holtzappel, "The Regional Governance Reform in Indonesia, 1999–2004", in *Decentralisation and Regional Autonomy in Indonesia*, edited by Holtzappel and Ramstedt.

18. M. Ryaas Rasyid, "Regional Autonomy and Local Politics in

Indonesia", in *Local Power and Politics in Indonesia: Decentralisation and Democratisation*, edited by Edward Aspinall and Greg Fealy (Singapore: Institute of Southeast Asian Studies and Centre for Strategic and International Studies, 2003), p. 63.

19. Ibid., p. 64.

20. The (almost) attempted coup by Lt General Prabowo against Habibie was a last minute, desperate attempt to restore military leadership over the state.

21. Correspondence with close advisor to Habibie during this period, August 2013.

22. Discussions with Srinavasan, 2007 and 2008.

23. Dewi Fortuna Anwar, "The Habibie Presidency: Catapulting Towards Reform", in *Soeharto's New Order and Its Legacy: Essays in Honour of Harold Crouch*, edited by Edward Aspinall and Greg Fealy (Canberra: ANU E-press, 2010), Chapter 7.

24. Pratikno,"Exercising freedom: Local autonomy and democracy in Indonesia", in *Regionalism in Post-Suharto Indonesia*, edited by Maribeth Erb, Priyambudi Sulistiyanto and Carole Faucher (RoutledgeCurzon, 2005), pp. 21–35.

25. For another analysis of this first phase of the post-Suharto period, see Olle Törnquist, "Dynamics of Indonesian Democratisation", *Third World Quarterly* 21, no. 3 (Jun 2000): 383–423. Törnquist's article is one of the most detailed analytical descriptions of the politics of 1998–2000. Törnquist correctly perceived that "First, while the politics of elite networks may remain, the centre has lost its grip and power (and the struggle for it) is now spreading to the provincial and local levels. This will therefore be the time of local politics." (p. 388). However, he did not, in that article, review the political economy of this. He continued: "Second, any new regime and any elite network need popular legitimacy. Hence, within the framework of more localised politics, this will also be the time of mass politics and elections." (p. 388). This was a partially correct formulation only. Mass politics has not yet appeared. Mass voter abstention has appeared instead. The slow emergence of mass politics is not so much a reflection of the weakness of political institutions, but of the difficulty after a long period of near totalitarian suppression of political life at the mass level, for mass participation to revive.

I discuss the re-emergence of labour politics in the final section of this essay.

26. Considerable useful data on the role of the ADB has been collated by the Institute of Global Justice in Jakarta in "Peran Asing Dalam Desentralisasi di Indonesia".

27. "List and sketches of parties", Agence France Presse, 17 May 1999.

28. <http://www.suarapembaruan.com/News/1999/10/261099/Politik/po01/po01.html>, Wed, 27 October 1999, 15:59:00 EDT.

"adanya negara federasi sangat diperlukan untuk mengatasi berbagai masalah fundamental, yaitu ketimpangan dalam bidang sosial, ekonomi, politik serta budaya. Untuk itu wacana negara federasi diperlukan dalam kerangka pemulihan hak asasi manusia (HAM) erta membangun perimbangan antara pusat dan daerah."

"Pembagian hasil (revenue sharing) antara pusat dan daerah sangat timpang. Kekayaan alam daerah sangat sedikit dirasakan oleh daerah penghasil. Dengan KKN-nya, pemerintah pusat mendapatkan terlalu besar dari hasil tersebut."

"Opsi selanjutnya adalah sistem federal... merupakan opsi tengah sekaligus 'jalan emas' yang mungkin paling baik untuk menyelesaikan masalah ketidakpuasan daerah."

29. <http://www.suaramerdeka.com/harian/9911/18/nas4.htm>, Wed, 17 November 1999, 15:57:00 EST. "Pertama, mempertahankan bentuk negara kesatuan, yakni ada konsentrasi kekuasaan luar biasa di Jakarta yang menumbuhkan eksploitasi luar Jawa oleh Jakarta dan menimbulkan KKN di mana-mana. 'Sudahlah, kita ucapkan selamat tinggal, harus ada perbaikan,' tegas dia, sambil menyatakan jika memaksakan diri untuk empertahankan bentuk negara kesatuan, Indonesia akan kolaps."

30. Ibid.

"Kalau referendum yang semangatnya memilih dua opsi, yaitu federasi atau otonomi seluas-luasnya, harus dilakukan secara nasional karena hal itu menyangkut bentuk negara."

31. "DPRD Kaltim Desak Pembentukan Negara Federal", Kompas, 11 November 1999.

32. These too were responses to "financial discrimination" not a sense of suppression of ethnic identity. In her chapter on the Riau region,

Michelle Ford concluded that a major escalation of conflict based on ethnic identity had been overstated. Ford, " Who are the Orang Riau? Negotiating identity across geographic and ethnic divides", in *Local Power and Politics in Indonesia*, edited by Aspinall and Fealy, p. 148.

33. George Quinn, "Coming apart and staying together at the centre: Debates over Provincial status in Java and Madura", in *Local Power and Politics in Indonesia*, edited by Aspinall and Fealy, pp. 164–78. This is an early discussion of this process on Java.

34. "Summary of the Amendments of the 1945 Constitution on State, Presidency and Region", in *Decentralization and Regional Autonomy in Indonesia*, edited by Holtzappel and Ramstedt, p. 54.

35. Ibid.

36. <http://us.politik.news.viva.co.id/news/read/396823-prabowo--pilkada-langsung-sarat-money-politics>.

   "Bahwa pilkada langsung ini kabupaten dan gubernur ini menurut saya harus dipikirkan bersama kembali, apakah tidak terlalu boros sebagai bangsa.... Saya berfikir pilkada gubernur dan bupati ini harus ditinjau kembali, mungkin tetap di DPRD sistem tidak rahasia, anggota DPRD yang tepilih untuk memilih bupati dia harus berdiri, jadi rakyat akan lihat wakil saya yang saya utus dia memilih bener atau tidak."

37. <http://data.worldbank.org/indicator/NY.GDP.MKTP.CD>.

38. <http://data.worldbank.org/indicator/NY.GDP.PCAP.CD>.

39. UNIDO, *Indonesia: Strategies for Manufacturing Competitiveness* (Jakarta, 2000), p. 30.

40. Ibid., p. 32.

41. Ibid., p. 33.

42. D. Bellefleur, Z. Murad and P. Tangkau, "A Snapshot of Indonesian Entrepreneurship and Micro, Small, and Medium Sized Enterprise Development", accessed from <http://setkab.go.id/lombaesai/files/data-statistik/penelitian-usaid-umkm-kur.pdf>.

43. There needs to be a broader theoretical discussion of the distinction between industry and simple manufacture. In much mainstream literature, including some posing as political economy, a crude division is accepted as to the sectors that contribute to the GDP: agriculture, finances and services, and "industry", sometimes

including, sometimes, excluding mining. A growth in the contribution of the "industry" sector to GDP and the expense of agriculture is often the basis for statements that a country has industrialized. Such an analysis is unacceptable crude and misleading. Manufacture preceded the industrial revolution in Europe. Industrial production introduced a revolutionary escalation in the level of mechanization, degree of specialization and scale of production. This intense mechanization and specialization alongside huge scale now dominates almost all production and distribution of goods and services in advanced industrial countries, including even in education and culture. It raises the average level of labour productivity dramatically and underpins the wealth of the industrial countries, alongside the exploitation of the rest of the world. In a country like Indonesia, these features of industrial production have hardly impacted on the society. The contribution of non-agricultural production to GDP has grown proportionally and this has changed Indonesian society dramatically. But it is not industrialization.

44. Richard Robison, *Indonesia: The Rise of Capital* (Jakarta: Equinox Publishing, 2009; 1st published 1986). See primarily Appendices.

45. See George Junus Aditjondro, *Korupsi Kepresidenan: Reproduksi Oligarki Berkaki Tiga – Istana, Tangsi, dan Parati Penguasa* (Yogyakarta: LKiS, 2006), pp. 2–23.

46. Ibid., pp. 377–85.

47. The 2013 listing can be found in *Globe Asia* 7, no. 6 (June 2013): 46–50.

48. For a summary of the immediate and devastating impact of all these agreements, see Roysepta Abimany, "Everlasting Woes", *Inside Indonesia* at <http://www.insideindonesia.org/feature-editions/everlasting-woes>.

49. I thank Nanang Indra Kurniawan for access to his research on Central Kalimantan in relation to this issue.

50. The nature of castes as a social layer in Indonesian society (inherited from pre-capitalist social formations) and their intersection with social classes (based on production relations) is a subject requiring urgent inquiry.

51. The first person to write in depth on the nature of the archipelago's

economy in the twentieth century emphasizing the smallness of scale of economic activity was Sukarno. He described how the specific character of Dutch imperialism gave everything "the stamp of smallness where ninety percent of which is composed of groups for whome everything is small, ... which a society has no industrial middle class, which is in the grip of a raw-materials imperialism and a capital-investment imperialism". Sukarno elaborated these ideas in one of his more extensive articles, "Swadesi and Mass Action in Indonesia", in *Under the Banner of the Revolution*, Vol. 1, 1966 and 2005, pp. 113–46. The quote is from p. 144. Given the population size, geographic spread and needs of Indonesia, the number of industrialists in Indonesian still remains insignificant.

52. According to University of Melbourne based researcher, Jess Melvin, her data even indicates a rapid growth in support for the PKI in Aceh throughout 1964.

53. An early contradictory manifestation of this bifurcation was the Sarekat Dagang Islam (and then Sarekat Islam [SI]) which flourished in the early twentieth century. It combined local small property owners and business people with a mass membership of workers and farmers. It took on a very "national", i.e., across the archipelago, scope. The membership was mobilized and politicized in anti-colonial activity. The alliance between the two class layers remained intact while the SI's political outlook remained primarily oppositional (to colonialism). When it needed to look to the future and decide what it stood forward programmatically, it split along class lines over the issues of the extent of its critique and opposition to capitalism. The leadership based amongst the merchant class, from an urban Islamic background, defended capitalism, the worker peasant membership, under the leadership of union leaders, broke away. The majority of the ideological descendants of the pro-capitalist wing of the SI were later to be found in the Masyumi party.

54. My formulation describing these events draws on John Roosa, *Pretext for Mass Murder: The September 30th Movement and Suharto's Coup d'État in Indonesia* (Madison: University of Wisconsin Press, 2006).

55. See the chapter "Memory", in Lane, *Unfinished Nation*.

56. Golkar was, of course, formed before 1965, on the initiative of the Armed Forces. It was at this time that the Army officer corps, many having been appointed as managers of nationalized (previously Dutch-owned) state enterprises, stated to develop class interests, related to their new business fiefdoms. Golkar was originally founded as the party of armed capitalists. See Max Lane, *Asal Usul Kediktatoran Kelas Orde Baru* (Jakarta, 1986).

57. See Edward Aspinall, *Opposing Suharto: Compromise, Resistance, and Regime Change In Indonesia* (Stanford: Stanford University Press, 2005), pp. 172–75.

58. This is contrary to some analysis that depicts the centralization as regional. "The main characteristics of this colonization have been: the imposition of a unique administrative model by centre-based administrators; a top-down developmental approach; and a policy of economic extraction to benefit the development of the central region, that is Java." Of course, the biggest conglomerates were based in Jakarta and Surabaya which are on the island of Java. However, it is a moot point indeed whether the vast majority of the people living on the island of Java will feel that they have been the beneficiaries of "development". Muriel Charras, "The reshaping of the Indonesian archipelago after 50 years of regional imbalance", in *Regionalism in Post-Suharto Indonesia*, edited by Erb, Sulistiyanto and Faucher.

59. Michael Buehler and Paige Johnson Tan, "Party-Candidate Relationships in Indonesian Local Politics: A Case Study of the 2005 Regional Elections In Gowa, South Sulawesi Province", *Indonesia* 84 (October 2007). Buehler also looks at the behaviour of the PKS's alliance with secular and Islamic parties in "Revisiting the inclusion-moderation thesis in the context of decentralized institutions: The behaviour of Indonesia's Prosperous Justice Party in national and local politics", in *Party Politics* 19, no. 2 (2012): 210–29.

60. Nankyung Choi, "Local Elections and Democracy in Indonesia: The Riau Archipelago", *Journal of Contemporary Asia* 37, no. 3 (August 2007): 326–45.

61. Michael Buehler, "Married with Children", *Inside Indonesia* 112, Apr–Jun 2013, <http://www.insideindonesia.org/feature-editions/married-with-children>.

62. See <http://hatta-rajasa.info/read/1316/masterplan-pembangunan-ala-hatta#sthash.90NZJi03.dpuf>.
63. Indonesia now has legally mandated free education for twelve years of schooling. As of 2014 a new social insurance law is in force that aims to deliver universal coverage. In both cases, there remain a range of issues which, for the time being, mean that the primary function of these welfare policies are as a social safety net for the most poor.
64. Thomas Pepinsky and Maria Wihardja, "Decentralization and Economic Performance in Indonesia", *Journal of East Asian Studies* 11 (2011): 337–71.
65. Ibid., p. 350.
66. Ibid., p. 352.
67. Ibid.
68. Ibid.
69. Ibid., p. 353.
70. Ibid., p. 358.
71. Ibid., p. 359.
72. Ibid., pp. 355–56.
73. Ministry of Home Affairs, Directorate General for Regional Autonomy, "Daftar Jumlah Provinsi, Kabupaten/Kota Seluruh Indonesia", at <http://otda.kemendagri.go.id/images/file/new_data/daftar%20jumlah%20prov.pdf>.
74. I thank here Nanang Indrakurniawan, Wawan Masudi and Ahyar Diar researchers at Victoria University, Melbourne, Australia, working on issues relating to local politics in Central and East Kalimantan and Central Java for the long discussions that have helped fill out a picture of these complicated processes.
75. Pepinsky and Wihardja, "Decentralization and Economic Performance in Indonesia", p. 360.
76. Buehler, "Revisiting the inclusion-moderation thesis".
77. Buehler, "Married with Children".
78. "Ribuan Pejabat Daerah Terlibat Kasus Korupsi", *Tempo*, 29 August 2012.
79. "Bupati-Bupati Luar Biasa, Korupsi Jadi Biasa", *Republika*, 24 December 2012.
80. I have not seen any calculations for the amount of money corrupted

at the *kabupaten* or municipal levels. Reports of scandals in the press point to amounts enough for the purchase of several properties, luxury cars and so on. Of course, these amounts are still far from enough to facilitate investment that would establish any significant twenty-first century industrial production. In this sense, this money rarely becomes capital, i.e., money used for productive investment, however measured.

81. I thank here Nanang Indrakurniawan, Wawan Masudi and Ahyar Diar researchers at Victoria University, Melbourne, Australia working on issues relating to local politics in Central and East Kalimantan and Central Java for the long discussions that have helped fill out a picture of these complicated processes.

82. Bert Hofman, Kai Kaiser, and Gunther G. Schulze, "Corruption and Decentralization", in *Decentralization and Regional Autonomy in Indonesia*, edited by Holtzappel and Ramstedt, p. 110.

83. Although at the local level, in some areas, the separation of business and local officialdom has disappeared.

84. Hofman, Kaiser, and G. Schulze, "Corruption and Decentralization", p. 111.

85. Ibid., p. 110.

86. Ibid.

87. Pepinsky and Wihardja, "Decentralization and Economic Performance in Indonesia", p. 364.

88. Ibid.

89. Ethnic attentions can become focused within local communities in this new context.

90. George Quinn, "Coming apart and staying together at the centre: Debates over Provincial status in Java and Madura", in *Local Power and Politics in Indonesia*, edited by Aspinall and Fealy, pp. 164–78.

91. As noted earlier, capital accumulation at this level is no where near enough, even after primitive accumulation, to engage in serious manufacturing, let alone, industrial investment.

92. It is interesting that some existing substantial nationally organized civic organizations have not emerged to play a role as a agency of political transformation. The two most obvious are Muhammadiyah and Nahdlatul Ulama. Muhammadiyah had a more national spread and a wider range of social welfare and educational activities.

Nahdlatul Ulama has a more significant regional bias, in East Java. However, neither organizations have deployed their considerable social infrastructure as part of acting as a political agency for national political change. Muhammadiyah has the most established infrastructure — schools, universities, hospitals, clinics, orphanages as well as an extensive branch system — with a national spread. But it has not been deployed politically behind any identifiable development perspective. The urban modernist Islamic political constituency has also fragmented, divided electorally among at least five parties. This fracturing may also be part of a regionalization or localization of this constituency's political life. It will be interesting to see whether the 2014 parliamentary elections reveal that these five parties have an increasingly region-centred voter support base.

93. It is difficult at this moment to identify the preferences of the U.S. government and elite in terms of the next Indonesian government, beyond such statements as the one below in support of Prabowo. One suspects these come from the harder, more conservative elements in U.S. politics. In many ways, Joko Widodo reflects — on paper — the candidate most qualified. He does not question current neo-liberalistic approach to economic policy but also supports a populist style of communication to profile social safety net policies, as well as so-called "transparency" and "good governance". He is a good "social peace" politician that may appeal to larger foreign capital in the factory belt areas. But perhaps, the social peace approach may not be adequate to pacify rising labour militancy.

94. Stanley Weiss, "Prabowo Could Be Indonesia's Lee Kuan Yew", *Huffington Post*, 28 September 2013 <http://www.huffingtonpost. com/stanley-weiss/prabowo-could-be-indonesi_b_3936498.html>.

95. I thank Wawan Masudi, researcher at Victoria University, Melbourne, Australia for access to his research data on Joko Widodo's career in Solo.

96. For a recent attempt to remedy this, see Ian Wilson, "Floods, housing security and rights of Jakarta's poor", *Jakarta Post*, 8 February 2013 <http://m.thejakartapost.com/news/2014/02/08/floods-housing-security-and-rights-jakarta-s-poor.html>.

97. <http://megapolitan.kompas.com/read/2013/05/21/1145411/Ini. Isi.Kontrak.Politik.Jokowi.kepada.Warga.Waduk>.

98. <http://www.merdeka.com/politik/ini-17-butir-rekomendasi-hasil-rakernas-iii-pdip-2013/rekomendasi-butir-1-6.html>.

99. "Sofjan Wanandi: Soal Upah, Buruh Jangan Ribut Dulu", Kompas. com, 26 September 2013 <http://bisniskeuangan.kompas.com/read/2013/09/26/1511461/Sofjan.Wanandi.Soal.Upah.Buruh. Jangan.Ribut.Dulu>.

100. In February 2014 somebody tweeted that the PDI-P had chosen Joko Widodo as presidential candidate and Puan Maharani, Megawati's daughter and a PDI-P leader, as vice-presidential candidate. The tweet received around 70,000 supporters. A few days later, somebody counter-tweeted saying that the PDI-P had chosen Joko Widodo and Rieke Pitaloka. This tweet received more than 1.2 million tweets of support within several hours.

101. Aspinall, "The Politics of Studying Indonesian Politics", in Knowing Indonesia, edited by Purdey, p. 70. This chapter is also available online at <http://books.publishing.monash.edu/apps/bookworm/view/Knowing+Indonesia%3A+Intersections+of+Self%2C+Discipline+and+Nation/177/OEBPS/c04.htm>.

102. Hadiz, Localising Power in Post-Authoritarian Indonesia, pp. 145–57.

103. For an alternative view on the role of labour in the transition from the New Order to the reformasi period, see Max Lane, "Indonesia and the Fall of Suharto: Proletarian Politics In The 'Planet Of Slums' Era", Working USA Journal of Labor and Society 13, Issue 2 (June 2010): 185–200.

104. Hadiz, Localising Power in Post-Authoritarian Indonesia, p. 151.

105. Ibid., p. 156.

106. The material in this section is based on interviews with trade union activists in Indonesia in January and April 2013. Material in the publication Majalah Sedane <http://www.majalahsedane.net/> has been invaluable.

107. The FSPMI, although now with a very different leadership, can also trace its origins back to the metal union inside the SPSI.

108. See also <http://www.majalahsedane.net/2012/09/danial-indrakusuma.html>.

109. Indrakusuma was a co-editor of the first left magazine of the late Suharto era, Progres, until it was banned in 1992, and one of the founders of the Peoples' Democratic Party (PRD) at about the same

time. He left the PRD not long before the expulsion of those in PRD in 2007, opposed to the rightward drift under the then Dita Sari leadership. Indrakusuma was also a critic of this direction. Sari is now a spokesperson for the Minister for Labour in the Yudhoyono government and has been campaigning to convince workers not to strike. Indrakusuma worked with others expelled from the PRD to form what is now the Peoples Liberation Party (PPR). However, he has been active outside the party for the last two years as a teacher of economics and politics for members of the FSPMI. He has become a popular figure among many workers who have been in his classes or read his ideas on union tactics. Since 2011 (at least) he has publicly advocated for a new workers' party.

110. See Michele Ford, "Employer Anti-Unionism in Democratic Indonesia", in *Global Anti-Unionism: Nature, Dynamics, Trajectories and Outcomes*, edited by Gregor Gall and Tony Dundon (Basingstoke: Palgrave Macmillan, 2013), pp. 224–43. This article provides some additional data on anti-union practices in the period up until around 2008. It concludes, however, with the rather banal and obvious statement: "And in the absence of meaningful checks and balances on employer behaviour, employers will continue to use strategies of containment, overt union busting and union busting by stealth designed to maximise their managerial discretion and minimise the challenge presented by organised labour." (p. 240).

111. Translated and abridged from extensive notes provided by Sherr Rinn, editor of the news website of the Miscellaneous Workers Union of Indonesia (SPAI) during 2012.

112. "Perihal: Undangan Konsolidasi Nasional", letter from Komite Persiapan Konsolidasi Nasional, dated 25 September 2013.

113. The chairperson of KSPI is Said Iqbal who is also chairperson of FSPMI.

114. "Daftar Undangan Aliansi/Organisasi Buruh", in "Perihal: Undangan Konsolidasi Nasional" letter.

References

Aditjondro, George Junus. *Korupsi Kepresidenan: Reproduksi Oligarki Berkaki Tiga — Istana, Tangsi, dan Parati Penguasa*. Yogyakarta: LKiS Yogyakarta, 2006.

Anwar, Dewi Fortuna: "The Habibie Presidency: Catapulting Towards Reform". In *Soeharto's New Order and Its Legacy: Essays in Honour of Harold Crouch*, edited by Edward Aspinall and Greg Fealy, Chapter 7. Canberra: ANU Epress, 2010.

Aspinall, Edward. *Opposing Suharto: Compromise, Resistance, and Regime Change in Indonesia*. Stanford: Stanford University Press, 2005.

———. "The Politics of Studying Indonesian Politics: Intellectuals, Political Research and Public Debate in Australia". In *Knowing Indonesia: Intersections of Self, Discipline and Nation*, edited by Jemma Purdey. Clayton: Monash University Publications, 2012.

——— and Greg Fealy. *Local Power and Politics in Indonesia: Decentralisation and Democratisation*. Singapore: Institute of Southeast Asian Studies and Centre for Strategic and International Studies, 2003.

Bellefleur, D., Z. Murad and P. Tangkau. "A Snapshot of Indonesian Entrepreneurship and Micro, Small, and Medium Sized Enterprise Development". Accessed from <http://setkab.go.id/lombaesai/files/data-statistik/penelitian-usaid-umkm-kur.pdf>.

Buehler, Michael. "Revisiting the inclusion-moderation thesis in the context of decentralized institutions: The behavior of Indonesia's Prosperous Justice Party in national and local politics". *Party Politics* 19, no. 2 (2012): 210–29.

———. "Married with Children", in *Inside Indonesia* 112 (Apr–Jun 2013). Accessed from <http://www.insideindonesia.org/feature-editions/married-with-children>.

119

————— and Paige Johnson Tan. "Party-Candidate Relationships In Indonesian Local Politics: A Case Study Of The 2005 Regional Elections in Gowa, South Sulawesi Province". *Indonesia* 84 (October 2007).

Charras, Muriel. "The reshaping of the Indonesian archipelago after 50 years of regional imbalance". In *Regionalism in Post-Suharto Indonesia*, edited by Maribeth Erb, Priyambudi Sulistiyanto and Carole Faucher. RoutledgeCurzon, 2005.

Choi, Nankyung. "Local Elections and Democracy in Indonesia: The Riau Archipelago". *Journal of Contemporary Asia* 37, no. 3 (Aug 2007): 326–45.

"Format Daerah Otonomi Indonesia (Laporan Akhir Penilitian)". Ilmu Pemerintahan, Universitas Gadjah Mada, 1997.

Hadiz, Vedi. *Localising Power in Post-Authoritarian Indonesia: A Southeast Asia Perspective*. Stanford: Stanford University Press, 2010.

————— and Richard Robison. *Reorganising Power in Indonesia: the Politics of Oligrachy in an Age of Markets*. New York: Routledge, 2004.

Hofman, Bert, Kai Kaiser and Gunther G. Schulze. "Corruption and Decentralization". In *Decentralization and Regional Autonomy in Indonesia: Implementation and Challenges*, edited by Coen J.G. Holtzappel and Martin Ramstedt. Singapore: Institute of Southeast Asian Studies and IIAS, 2009.

Holtzappel, Coen J. G. "The Regional Governance Reform in Indonesia, 1999–2004". In *Decentralization and Regional Autonomy in Indonesia: Implementation and Challenges*, edited by Coen J.G. Holtzappel and Martin Ramstedt. Singapore: Institute of Southeast Asian Studies and IIAS, 2009.

————— and Martin Ramstedt, eds. *Decentralization and Regional Autonomy in Indonesia: Implementation and Challenges*. Singapore: Institute of Southeast Asian Studies and IIAS, 2009.

Karim, Abdul Gaffar. *Kompleksitas Persoalan Otonomi Daerah di Indonesia*. Yogyakarta: Jurusan Ilmu Pemerintahan, Universitas Gadjah Mada and Pustaka Pelajar, 2003.

Lane, Max. *Asal Usul Kediktatoran Kelas Orde Baru*. Jakarta, 1986.

—————. *Unfinished Nation: Indonesia Before and After Suharto*. London and New York: Verso, 2008.

—————. "Indonesia and the Fall of Suharto: Proletarian Politics in the

'Planet of Slums' Era". *Working USA Journal of Labor and Society* 13, Issue 2 (June 2010): 185–200.

Law No. 32/2004 on the Fiscal Balance of Regional Administration. Available in *Decentralization and Regional Autonomy in Indonesia: Implementation and Challenges*, edited by Coen J.G. Holtzappel and Martin Ramstedt, pp. 49–51. Singapore: Institute of Southeast Asian Studies and IIAS, 2009.

Ministry of Home Affairs, Directorate General for Regional Autonomy. "Daftar Jumlah Provinsi, Kabupaten/Kota Seluruh Indonesia". Available at <http://otda.kemendagri.go.id/images/file/new_data/daftar%20jumlah%20prov.pdf>.

National Committee for DEMOCRATIC Struggle. "Form a council of political leaders to safeguard the sovereignty of the people!". January 1998.

Pepinsky, Thomas and Maria Wihardja. "Decentralization and Economic Performance in Indonesia". *Journal of East Asian Studies* 11 (2011): 337–71.

PIJAR's Tritura 1998. Posted by Tapol, 11 January 1998.

Pratikno. "Exercising freedom: Local autonomy and democracy in Indonesia". In *Regionalism in Post-Suharto Indonesia*, edited by Maribeth Erb, Priyambudi Sulistiyanto and Carole Faucher, pp. 21–35. RoutledgeCurzon, 2005.

Quinn, George. "Coming apart and staying together at the centre: Debates over Provincial status in Java and Madura". In *Local Power and Politics in Indonesia: Decentralisation and Democratisation*, edited by Edward Aspinall and Greg Fealy. Singapore: Institute of Southeast Asian Studies and Centre for Strategic and International Studies, 2003.

Robison, Richard. *Indonesia: The Rise of Capital*. Jakarta: Equinox Publishing, 2009; 1st published 1986.

Sidel, John. "Bossism and democracy in the Philippines, Thailand, and Indonesia: Towards an alternative framework for the study of 'local strongmen'". In *Politicising Democracy: The New Local Politics of Democratisation*, edited by John Harriss, Kristin Stokke and Olle Tornquist. International Political Economy Series, pp. 51–74. Basingstoke: Palgrave Macmillan, 2004.

Suharyo, Widjajanti I. "Indonesia's Transition to Decentralised Governance: Evolution at the Local Level". In *Decentralization and*

Regional Autonomy in Indonesia: Implementation and Challenges, edited by Coen J.G. Holtzappel and Martin Ramstedt, pp. 75–98. Singapore: Institute of Southeast Asian Studies and IIAS, 2009.

UNIDO. *Indonesia: Strategies for Manufacturing Competitiveness*. Jakarta, 2000.

VISI calon presiden RI , 26 February 1998 23:56:56 PST, <http://www.library.ohiou.edu/indopubs/1998/02/28/0076.html>.

Weiss, Stanley. "Prabowo Could Be Indonesia's Lee Kuan Yew". *Huffington Post*, 28 September 2013 <http://www.huffingtonpost.com/stanley-weiss/prabowo-could-be-indonesi_b_3936498.html>.

Wignusubroto, Soetandya et al. *Pasang Surut Otonomi Daerah Sketsa Perjalanan 100 Tahun*. Jakarta: Institute for Local Development and Yayasan TIFA, November, 2005.